Grammar Rulz!

Daily practice • Social studies themes • Tech-friendly

Erik Ortman

Grammar Rulz!
Daily practice • Social studies themes • Tech-friendly

By Erik Ortman

Cover design: Studio Montage
Illustrations: Martina Mizraje
Back cover and book design: Mickey Cuthbertson

Library of Congress Cataloging-in-Publication Data

Ortman, Erik.
 Grammar rulz! : daily practice, social studies themes, tech-friendly /
Erik Ortman.
    p. cm.
 Includes bibliographical references.
 ISBN-13: 978-1-934338-65-0 (pbk.)
 ISBN-10: 1-934338-65-6 (pbk.)
 1. English language--Grammar--Study and teaching (Middle school) 2.
Social sciences--Study and teaching (Middle school) I. Title. II.
Title: Grammar rules!
 LB1631.O78 2010
 428.2071'2--dc22
                        2010002607

Maupin House publishes professional resources for K-12 educators. Contact us for tailored, in-school training or to schedule an author for a workshop or conference.
Visit www.maupinhouse.com for free lesson plan downloads.

Maupin House Publishing, Inc.
2416 NW 71st Place
Gainesville, FL 32653
www.maupinhouse.com
800-524-0634
352-373-5588
352-373-5546 (fax)
info@maupinhouse.com

10 9 8 7 6 5 4 3 2 1

In memory of
Chris Heim and Martin Rawley

Acknowledgements

It's a pleasure to recognize the contributions of the many people who assisted with this project. Hugs and kisses to Larisa and Jack for their support throughout. My deepest appreciation to Karla Sutton for her inspiration, constant encouragement, knowledgeable advice, and technical expertise. Special recognition to Martina Mizraje, a talented young artist, for her work on illustrations. Much appreciation is also due to Andrea Paola Campos, for her kind assistance and support. Thanks to Emily Raij for her tireless editing and thoughtful suggestions, to Tiffany Morgan for her insight and helpful comments, and to Mickey Cuthbertson for his creative talents. Cheers to Alexandra Baines, for her clever ideas regarding program use and medieval history. Finally, in the place of honor, a special thanks to my students.

Table of Contents

Introduction

Answer Keys

CD Contents

(Folder) Student Exercises and Answer Keys

Chapter One—The Forgotten Pharaoh
- PDF version
- SMART Board® version
- Mimio® version
- *Grammar Rulz* Express Student Packet
- Character 'TOONS

Chapter Two—The Ancient Geeks
- PDF version
- SMART Board® version
- Mimio® version
- *Grammar Rulz Express* Student Packet
- Character 'TOONS

Chapter Three—Trouble at Vesuvius
- PDF version
- SMART Board® version
- Mimio® version
- *Grammar Rulz* Express Student Packet
- Character 'TOONS

Chapter Four—Anne and the Vikings
- PDF version
- SMART Board® version
- Mimio® version
- *Grammar Rulz* Express Student Packet
- Character 'TOONS

Bonus Chapter—Sunset High School
- PDF version
- SMART Board® version
- Mimio® version
- *Grammar Rulz* Express Student Packet
- Character 'TOONS

(Folder) Instructional Videos
- *Grammar Rulz* Overview Video
- SMART Board® Video
- SMART Screen Capture Video
- Mimio® Interactive Systems Video
- Mimio® Screen Clipping Video
- PDF Video
- Assessment Video

(Folder) Bonus Materials
- Printable SUPER PROOFER proofreading symbols placard
- My Spelling Gremlins personal spelling list
- Middle School Writing Standards
- Punctuation Nation (nine printable placards)

Introduction

Author's Note

Each August, I unlock a dusty bookroom and stand for a while among shelves crowded with myths, novels, and anthologies that students have enjoyed over the years. These books mark out the pleasant milestones of a school year to come, but my eyes inevitably settle on the largest stacks in the room: enormous piles of grammar textbooks. Certainly these books contain much that should be taught, yet I've always wished for another way.

The appearance of any grammar text—ours run to more than 700 pages—in a classroom can cause dread, occasional nosebleeds, and a noticeable spike in bathroom visits; nevertheless, the writing conventions (spelling, capitalization, punctuation, grammar, and usage) typically covered by grammar textbooks remain cornerstones of literacy. Thus, the light use of a grammar text serves as a sensible complement to teaching grammar in context and school-wide agreements that ask the entire faculty to focus on effective writing. Beyond that, daily language exercises like *Grammar Rulz* are an efficient way to address writing mechanics and basic grammar while performing another rarely noted function: allowing teachers and students to have a sustained conversation about language. This is priceless.

Daily language exercises are mini-lessons that engage and focus students during those often unruly first moments of class when you're struggling to take attendance, collect late work, and remember where you left that stack of tests. Moreover, these starter exercises create a few tranquil minutes in which you can work individually with students. As a teacher in an urban public school, I found starters to be an invaluable classroom-management tool, but it was also delightful to discover they had a positive impact on student writing and standardized test scores. Soon, I began writing my own story-based starters. Essentially, these were short pieces of fiction set within whatever historical period my students were studying.

Grammar Rulz is the result of years of classroom experimentation, and over time it has produced notable results. When used consistently, the program can help students master basic writing conventions without morphing into glassy-eyed zombies. Lasting roughly six weeks, a typical unit allows students to follow the adventures of kids their own age while gaining valuable insight into how language works. Each day's exercise contains twelve errors and can be completed in as little as three minutes. There's also a pithy rule to cement understanding, an extension activity to augment concept mastery, a challenging vocabulary word, and two built-in assessments. In addition, *Grammar Rulz* provides teachers and students with a rich, authentic context in which to talk about written language.

Grammar Rulz is *not* a prescriptive battering ram. It is, I hope, an enjoyable vehicle through which you and your students can explore the marvelous subtlety and rich history of the English language. As the weeks tick past, I hope you'll find *Grammar Rulz* to be a helpful tool, an agreeable companion, and a pleasant moment in your school day.

— *Erik Ortman*

Grammar Rulz!

Example Exercise

Here's a typical *Grammar Rulz* exercise:

Twenty two Gladiator was fighting practice bouts with wooden weapons, training was going good when a tremor shaked the Earth.

"Oh no " I shreiked.

Grammar Boy sez,

Good is usually an adjective; *well* is usually an adverb.

Brain Blaster!

1. I have a _____ job, and it pays _____.

2. He writes _____; he's a _____ author.

3. I have _____ friends who treat me really _____.

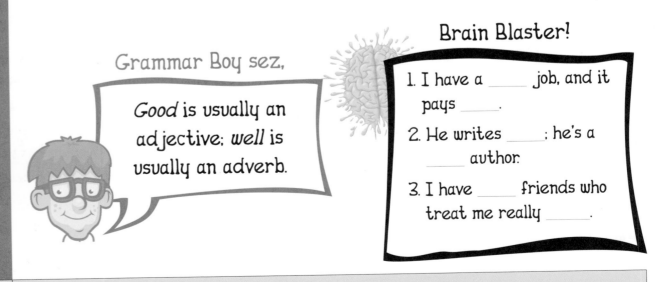

And here's an answer key:

Twenty two Gladiators were fighting practice bouts with wooden weapons. training was going well when a tremor shook the Earth. "Oh no!" I shreiked.

tremor (n.) – a slight shaking

Grammar Boy sez,

Good is usually an adjective; *well* is usually an adverb.

Brain Blaster!

1. I have a good job, and it pays well.

2. He writes well; he's a good author.

3. I have good friends who treat me really well.

Decision 1—Choose your presentation format

❏ **SMART Board®**—Open a preformatted SMART Notebook file from the CD to display *Grammar Rulz* exercises. Students (call them to the board in pairs) use SMART Board markers to make twelve changes directly on the screen before the teacher superimposes an answer key atop their work. *Grammar Rulz* and SMART Boards make a seamless match! See the detailed SMART Board instructions (pages xxii-xxiii) and the instructional videos on the CD for more details. You can also use SMART Notebook software's "area capture" feature to custom format *Grammar Rulz* exercises for use on your SMART Board system.

❏ **Mimio® interactive whiteboard**—Open preformatted Mimio files from the CD to display *Grammar Rulz* exercises on your Mimio interactive system. Students (call them to the board in pairs) use Mimio stylus pens to make twelve changes directly on the screen before the teacher superimposes an answer key atop their work. *Grammar Rulz* and Mimio interactive systems make a perfect pair! See the detailed Mimio instructions (pages xxiv-xxv) and the instructional videos on the CD for more details. You can also use Mimio Notebook software's "import file" (file > import) or "screen clipping" feature (Tools > Mimio Tools) to custom format *Grammar Rulz* exercises for use on your Mimio system.

❏ **Multimedia computer projector**—Open a chapter (in PDF format) from the CD to display *Grammar Rulz* exercises through your multimedia projector. Most teachers choose to aim their projector at a whiteboard, allowing students to make twelve corrections with dry-erase markers before the teacher superimposes an answer key atop student work.

❏ **Overhead projector**—Print black line masters from the CD to make transparencies of each day's exercise. Extension activities (Grammar Boy's rule and the Brain Blaster extension activity) are sized to let you cover them with 3" x 3" sticky notes so you can unveil them when the time comes. Many teachers aim their overhead projector at a whiteboard to allow students to make corrections with dry-erase markers. If no whiteboard is available, students can easily make corrections on the transparency itself.

❏ **Whiteboard**—Write the day's exercise on the board. As students complete the exercise at their desks, call a pair forward to share their corrections (in a contrasting color) at the board. At the end of each period, have a student copy the next exercise onto your whiteboard for the next class to use.

❏ **Chalkboard**—Write the day's exercise on the board. As students complete the exercise at their desks, call two students forward to make their corrections at the board. At the end of each period, have a student copy the next exercise onto your chalkboard for your next class to use.

Decision 2—Choose a response format for students

The Notebook Method (fast)—Have the day's exercise projected or written on the board. When students enter the classroom, they open their language arts notebooks, jot down the starter—rarely more than twenty-five words—and then make twelve corrections in a contrasting color. A sample notebook entry can be found below. In addition, a model and a practice exercise are located at the start of each chapter.

Sample *Grammar Rulz* notebook entry

Friday, October 13, 2006

dear John,

    I can't go with you to the halloween soiree. i'm going to the Dance with Lance.

sincerely not Yours,

Tyra

Grammar Boy sez,

"Capitalize holidays."

Brain Blaster

1. Groundhog Day
2. New Year's Day
3. April Fools' Day

The *Grammar Rulz* notebook method:

dear John

I can't go with you to the halloween soiree. i'm going to the Dance with Lance.

sincereley not Yours

Tyra

soiree (n.)

Define and sketch this word if you finish early.

Step 1 – **Write the exercise (including mistakes) in your notebook. Double spacing helps!**

Step 2 – **Use colorful ink to correct twelve mistakes with SUPER PROOFER proofreading symbols.**

Step 3 (optional) – **Jot down Grammar Boy's rule.**

Grammar Boy sez,

Capitalize holidays!

Step 4 (optional) – **Do the Brain Blaster extension exercise.**

Brain Blaster!

List 3 great holidays:
1. Groundhog Day
2. New Year's Day
3. April Fools' Day

Decision 2 (continued)—Choose a response format for students

The *Grammar Rulz* Express Method (wicked fast)—Have the day's exercise projected or written on the board. When students enter the classroom, they open their pre-printed *Grammar Rulz* Express packet (printable versions with two exercises per page can be found on the CD) and make twelve colorful corrections. A sample *Grammar Rulz* Express sheet can be found below. In addition, a model and a practice exercise are located at the start of each chapter.

Sample *Grammar Rulz* Express page

Alpha Date: Friday, 1 April 2011

A comotion waked zeus on the hieght of mount Olympus, his stern eyes sweeped over the mountainous greek countriside and come to rest on athens.

Grammar Boy sez,
"Capitalize the names of gods and deities."

Brain Blaster
Leader = Zeus
Queen = Hera
♡ = Aphrodite
Cupid = Eros
Messenger = Hermes
Music = Apollo

stern (adj.)- totally serious!

Beta Date: Monday, 4 April 2011

"Ugh, it's saturday morning and there hamering away on thier stupid acropolis over their," zeus mutered into his mamoth white beard.

Grammar Boy sez,
"There = yonder; theyre = they are; their shows ownership."

Brain Blaster
They're worried their old car won't make it there.

acropolis (n.)- A high place in an ancient Greek city state.

The *Grammar Rulz* Express method

1.   Date: <u>September 3, 2011</u>

dear John

   I can't go with you to the halloween soiree. i'm going to the Dance with Lance. sincereley not Yours, Tyra

Step 1 – **Use colored ink to correct twelve mistakes on a pre-printed *Grammar Rulz* Express packet.**

Step 2 – **Jot down Grammar Boy's rule.**

Step 3 – **Do the Brain Blaster exercise.**

<u>Grammar Boy sez,</u>
"Capitalize holidays!"

Define and sketch this word if you finish early.

soiree (n.)—**A party during the evening. It comes from *soir*, the French word for evening.**

<u>Brain Blaster!</u>
List 3 great holidays:
1. Groundhog Day
2. New Year's Day
3. April Fools' Day

Materials—Give 'em the tools for success!

Student Materials

✔ Brain

✔ A language arts notebook

✔ Two contrasting pen colors and a highlighter

✔ A list of SUPER PROOFER proofreading symbols (a printable version can be found on the CD) pasted or copied into their notebooks

✔ A My Spelling Gremlins list (printable versions can be found on the CD and at the end of each *Grammar Rulz* Express packet) pasted into their notebooks

✔ An optional but highly recommended *Grammar Rulz* Express packet (printable versions can be found on the CD)

✔ A dictionary at each desk or table

Teacher Materials

✔ Coffee

✔ A multimedia computer projector or SMART Board or Mimio interactive system or overhead projector or whiteboard or chalkboard

✔ Markers or chalk or SMART Board markers or Mimio stylus pens in three colors

✔ An optional but *highly recommended* CD/MP3 player with speakers. Use a catchy theme song that has to do with writing or the story. Play the music when two students come to the board or screen to make corrections for the class. A little music takes some of the sting out of grammar.

✔ Print and post the Punctuation Nation and SUPER PROOFER placards from the CD.

> Have some fun! Choose a cool theme song to go with the story.

Step 1—Review the writing conventions by asking students to trace their hands in their notebooks!

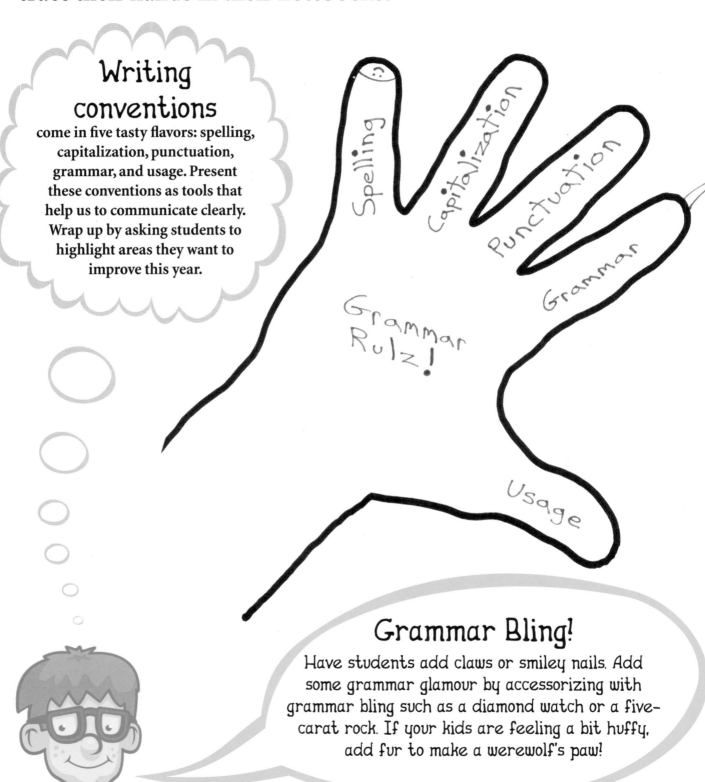

Writing conventions

come in five tasty flavors: spelling, capitalization, punctuation, grammar, and usage. Present these conventions as tools that help us to communicate clearly. Wrap up by asking students to highlight areas they want to improve this year.

Spelling

Capitalization

Punctuation

Grammar

Grammar Rulz!

Usage

Grammar Bling!

Have students add claws or smiley nails. Add some grammar glamour by accessorizing with grammar bling such as a diamond watch or a five-carat rock. If your kids are feeling a bit huffy, add fur to make a werewolf's paw!

Step 1 (continued)—Review writing conventions!

Students usually enjoy the previous goal-setting exercise (the hand thing), and you may gain some valuable insight by asking a few open-ended questions such as, "What areas do you find most difficult?" and, "What areas do you want to know more about?" If planets align above your classroom, a reckless student may venture, "What exactly is grammar?" Below, you'll find a few examples to help you through the moment.

Grammar. The word has sent chills up the spines of students for thousands of years, yet, simply put, grammar is little more than a set of shared ideas about how words and sentences are formed. Grammar helps us communicate complex ideas in crisp, elegant prose that informs, persuades, entertains, and enriches others.

Here's the good news: your students already know grammar. Prove it to them by writing this sentence on the board: ***Wants my brother to be a doctor witch.*** Now, ask them to fix it without adding any new words. With luck, most will recast the sentence in one of several equally upsetting but grammatically happier versions: ***My brother wants to be a witch doctor*** or ***A witch doctor wants to be my brother.*** Without being able to articulate it, most students know that the subject in the original sentence (*brother*) normally precedes the verb (*wants*), and they know that an adjective generally precedes the noun it modifies. This is grammar.

Should there arise an unlikely clamor for further examples, have students use dictionaries to add as many suffixes as humanly possible to a base word: *human.* Now explain, "The way we form words is also a part of grammar."

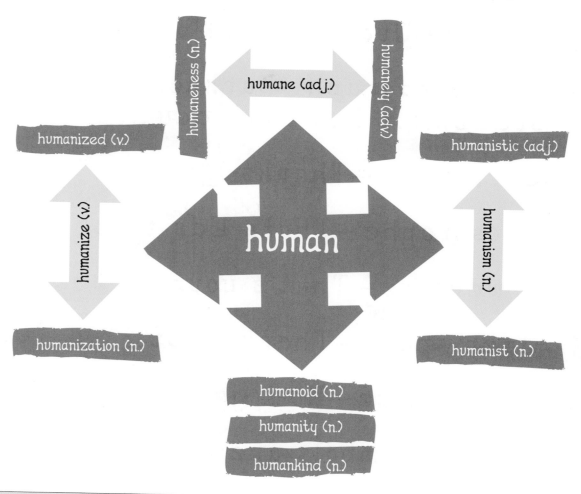

Step 2—Introduce proofreading symbols!
Students should paste these into their notebooks!

SUPER PROOFER PROOFREADING SYMBOLS

Comma—Dude, stop the insanity!

Reverse—Santa's riendeer too are sleepy to fly.

Delete—You're begginning to to reek!

Period—Mom just got paid. Let's order pizza!

Insert—Juana has a cute brother.

New paragraph—Darkness fell suddenly. The next day...

Capitalize—Thanks, dad.

Apostrophe—That's Eds taco!

Lowercase—That's your Sister?

Open space—Thanks alot.

Close space—Now, go a way!

Dotted symbols are optional.

Step 3—Run the three-minute drill!

BEFORE CLASS: Project or display the day's exercise.

BELL RINGS: As soon as they enter, students begin working on the exercise in their notebooks or packets.

2–3 MINUTES: After two or three minutes, call two students forward to share corrections as the others check their work. Briefly review the corrections before superimposing the answer key.

OPTIONAL: Students jot down Grammar Boy's rule and complete the Brain Blaster extension activity.

Step 4a.—Do it!

Instructions for SMART Board users

BEFORE CLASS

1. Calibrate your screen.

   OPTIONAL: Feeling the need for speed? Make back-to-back copies of the *Grammar Rulz* Express packet (found on the CD) for your students.

2. Use pre-formatted SMART Notebook files from the CD to display *Grammar Rulz* exercises on your SMART Board. Students use SMART Board markers to make changes directly on the screen before the teacher superimposes an answer key atop student work. See the instructional video on the CD for a demo. **If you want to keep it simple, skip to step 12.**

3. If you'd prefer to custom format your own SMART Notebook pages, open the CD and choose a *Grammar Rulz* chapter (in PDF format) you'd like to use. Every chapter starts with explanatory material, a model, and a practice exercise. On your PDF viewer's upper menu, choose the following: View > Page Display > Two-Up. The uncorrected exercise and the answer key should appear side by side. If they don't, go to your PDF viewer's upper menu and choose the following: View > Page Display > Show Cover Page During Two-Up. See the instructional video on the CD for a demo.

4. Use the zoom feature (50 percent works well) to display a complete side-by-side view of **both** the uncorrected exercise and answer key

5. Open your SMART Notebook software.

6. From the upper menu, choose the following: View > Screen Capture Toolbar. Ensure you click the "Save to new page" option.

7. Click back to the *Grammar Rulz* PDF file, and then use the screen capture tool to capture **both** the student exercise and answer key.

8. Return to the SMART Notebook page where you'll find the image you've just captured.

9. Click back to the *Grammar Rulz* PDF file, zoom in on Grammar Boy's rule and the Brain Blaster exercise, and then use the screen capture tool to capture it.

10. Return to the SMART Notebook page where you'll find the image you've just captured.

11. Repeat steps 7-9 until you've captured the entire chapter.

12. Choose View > Zoom > 200% so that students can only see the uncorrected exercise. You can also use the resizing handles (hold down the shift key) to ensure the uncorrected exercise fills the screen.

13. From the upper menu of the Smart Notebook document, choose the screen shade feature to use when you present Grammar Boy's rule and the Brain Blaster extension activity. See the instructional video on the CD for a SMART Board demo!

DURING CLASS

14. Every chapter starts with explanatory material, a model, and a practice exercise. Project the "Notebook Method" or "*Grammar Rulz* Express Method" page while you walk students through the method. Provide students with a copy, and have them highlight steps 1-4 along with the twelve corrections. Try out *Grammar Rulz* by doing the practice exercise together.

15. Project your first exercise. Adjust the zoom (200 or 300 percent) or resize the image while holding down the shift key. Tell students there are about twelve mistakes. A flexible number leaves wiggle room for disagreement on disputed points such as the final comma in a list of items. Circulate as students make corrections in their notebooks or *Grammar Rulz* Express packets or laptops or workstations. Then…

      • Hit the music

      • Call two students forward to make six corrections each (use any color but red)

      • Stop the music

      • Briefly review the corrections

16. After the review, put down the markers/eraser and drag the answer key over from the right until it aligns with student corrections. Before dragging, click on a blank space within the exercise (make sure the dotted box around the exercise pops up) to allow easy alignment.

17. **OPTIONAL:** Reveal Grammar Boy's rule with the screen shade feature. Ask students to jot it in their notebooks or *Grammar Rulz* Express packets. Pressed for time or unsure about a rule? Don't sweat it—skip it!

18. **OPTIONAL:** Reveal the Brain Blaster extension to reinforce the rule. The word of the day (right margin) offers additional extension for those who finish early.

19. Have your next *Grammar Rulz* exercise projected when students enter the following day.

Note: See the "Tips for Success" section for a detailed look at best practices.

Step 4b.—Do it!

Instructions for Mimio interactive system users

BEFORE CLASS

1. Calibrate your screen before opening the CD to choose a pre-formatted Mimio chapter to display on your interactive whiteboard. Students use Mimio stylus markers to make corrections directly on the screen before the teacher superimposes an answer key atop student work. See the instructional video on the CD for a demo. Every chapter starts with explanatory material. **If you want to keep it simple, skip to step 11.**

   OPTIONAL: Feeling the need for speed? Make back-to-back copies of the *Grammar Rulz* Express packet (found on the CD) for your students.

2. If you'd prefer to custom format your own Mimio pages, open the CD and choose a *Grammar Rulz* chapter (in PDF format) you'd like to use. On your PDF viewer's upper menu, choose the following: View > Page Display > Two-Up. The uncorrected exercise and the answer key should appear side by side. If they don't, go to your PDF viewer's upper menu and choose the following: View > Page Display > Show Cover Page During Two-Up.

3. Use the zoom feature (50 percent works well) to display a complete side-by-side view of both the uncorrected exercise and answer key.

4. Open your Mimio Notebook software.

5. From the upper menu, choose the following: Tools > Mimio tools.

6. Click back to the *Grammar Rulz* PDF file, and then use the screen clipping tool to capture both the student exercise and answer key for the *Grammar Rulz* exercise.

7. Return to the Mimio Notebook page where you'll find the image you've captured.

8. Click back to the *Grammar Rulz* PDF file, zoom in on Grammar Boy's rule and the Brain Blaster exercise, and then use the screen clipping tool to capture it.

9. Return to the Mimio Notebook page where you'll find the image you've captured.

10. Repeat steps 7-9 until you've captured the entire chapter.

11. Zoom in so that students can only see the uncorrected exercise. You can also use the resizing handles (hold down the shift key) to ensure the uncorrected exercise fills the screen.

12. From the Mimio Tools menu, choose Applications > Reveal to use the shade feature when you present Grammar Boy's rule and the Brain Blaster extension activity. See the instructional video on the CD for a Mimio interactive system demo!

DURING CLASS

13. Every chapter starts with explanatory material, a model, and a practice exercise. Project the "Notebook Method" or "*Grammar Rulz* Express Method" page while you walk students through the method. Provide students with a copy, and have them highlight steps 1-4 along with the twelve corrections. Try out *Grammar Rulz* by doing the practice exercise together.

14. Project your first exercise. Adjust the zoom or resize the image while holding down the shift key. Tell students there are about twelve mistakes. A flexible number leaves wiggle room for disagreement on disputed points such as the final comma in a list of items. Circulate as students make corrections in their notebooks or *Grammar Rulz* Express packets or laptops or workstations. Then...

    • Hit the music

    • Call two students forward to make six corrections each (use any color but red)

    • Stop the music

    • Briefly review the corrections

15. After the review, drag the answer key over from the right until it aligns with student corrections. Before dragging, click on a blank space within the exercise (make sure the dotted box around the exercise pops up) to allow easy alignment.

16. **OPTIONAL:** Reveal Grammar Boy's rule with the screen shade feature. Ask students to jot it in their notebooks or *Grammar Rulz* Express packets. Pressed for time or unsure about a rule? Don't sweat it— skip it!

17. **OPTIONAL:** Reveal the Brain Blaster extension to reinforce the rule. The word of the day (right margin) offers additional extension for those who finish early.

18. Have your next *Grammar Rulz* exercise projected when students enter the following day.

Note: See the "Tips for Success" section for a detailed look at best practices.

Step 4c.—Do it!

Instructions for multimedia computer projector users

1. Open the CD and choose a *Grammar Rulz* PDF file. Every chapter starts with explanatory material, a model, and a practice exercise. Project the "Notebook Method" or "*Grammar Rulz* Express Method" page on your whiteboard or screen while you walk students through the method. Provide students with a copy, and have them highlight steps 1-4 along with the twelve corrections. Try out *Grammar Rulz* by doing the practice exercise together.

2. **OPTIONAL:** Feeling the need for speed? Make back-to-back copies of the *Grammar Rulz* Express packets for your students to write on directly.

3. Project your first *Grammar Rulz* exercise. Adjust the zoom (110 percent, etc.) so students can see the exercise but not the Grammar Boy or Brain Blaster sections. Tell students there are about twelve mistakes. A flexible number leaves wiggle room for disagreement on disputed points such as the final comma in a list of items. Circulate as students make corrections in their notebooks or *Grammar Rulz* Express packets.

4a. If you're projecting on a whiteboard...	4b. If you're projecting on a screen...
o Hit the music o Call two students to the whiteboard to make six corrections each (have students use any color but red) o Stop the music o Briefly review the corrections o Project the answer key atop the students' corrections.	o Display the answer key o Briefly review the corrections o As you can see at left, aiming your projector at a whiteboard generates tons of interactivity...

5. **OPTIONAL:** Adjust your zoom (300 percent works well) and use the Hand Tool to fill the screen with Grammar Boy's rule. Ask students to jot it in their notebooks or *Grammar Rulz* Express packets. Pressed for time or unsure about a rule? Don't sweat it—skip it!

6. **OPTIONAL:** Reduce your zoom (150 percent works well) to reveal the Brain Blaster extension and reinforce the rule. The word of the day (right margin) offers additional extension for students who finish early.

7. Have your next *Grammar Rulz* exercise projected when students enter the next day.

Note: See the "Tips for Success" section for a detailed look at best practices.

Step 4d.—Do it!

Instructions for overhead projector users

1. Select a chapter. Print black line masters from the CD to make transparencies of each day's exercise and any examples or practice exercises (found at the beginning of each CD chapter) you'd like to use.

2. **OPTIONAL:** Feeling the need for speed? Make back-to-back copies of the *Grammar Rulz* Express packets for your students.

3. Project the "Notebook Method" or "*Grammar Rulz* Express Method" (pages 14-16) on your whiteboard or screen while you walk students through the steps. Provide students with a hard copy, and have them highlight steps 1-4 along with the twelve corrections. Try out *Grammar Rulz* by doing the practice exercise together.

4. Many teachers aim an overhead projector at a whiteboard to allow students to make corrections with dry erase markers, but take care that everyone avoids looking into the projector light. If no whiteboard is available, students can easily make corrections for the class on the transparency itself.

5. Cover the Grammar Boy and Brain Blaster sections with sticky notes.

6. Project a practice exercise or your first *Grammar Rulz* exercise. Tell students there are about twelve mistakes. A flexible number leaves wiggle room for disagreement on disputed points such as the final comma in a list of items. Circulate as students make corrections in their notebooks or packets.

7a. If you're projecting on a whiteboard…	7b. If you're projecting on a screen…
o Hit the music o Call two students to the whiteboard to make six corrections each o Stop the music o Briefly review the corrections	o Hit the music o Call two students to the overhead to make six corrections each on the transparency. o Stop the music o Briefly review the corrections

8. **OPTIONAL:** Reveal Grammar Boy's rule, and have students jot it in their notebooks or packets. Pressed for time or unsure about a rule? Don't sweat it—skip it!

9. **OPTIONAL:** Do the Brain Blaster extension to reinforce the rule. The word of the day (right margin) offers additional extension for students who finish early.

10. Have your next *Grammar Rulz* exercise projected when students enter the next day.

Note: See the "Tips for Success" section for a detailed look at best practices.

Step 4e.—Do it!

Instructions for whiteboard or chalkboard users

Note: The *Grammar Rulz* Express method is particularly helpful for chalkboard and whiteboard users!

1. Every chapter starts with explanatory material, a model, and a practice exercise. Make copies of the "Notebook Method" or "*Grammar Rulz* Express Method" page and walk students through the steps. Try out *Grammar Rulz* by doing the practice exercise together.

2. **OPTIONAL:** Feeling the need for speed? Make back-to-back copies of the *Grammar Rulz* Express packets for your students.

3. Write your first *Grammar Rulz* exercise (big, colorful, and bold) on your board. Tell students there are about twelve mistakes. A flexible number leaves wiggle room for disagreement on disputed points such as the final comma in a list of items. Circulate as students make corrections in their notebooks or *Grammar Rulz* Express packets.

   - Hit the music (have markers/chalk ready)
   - Call two students to the board to make six corrections each
   - Stop the music

4. Review the corrections.

5. **OPTIONAL:** Write down Grammar Boy's rule on your board. Ask students to jot it in their notebooks or *Grammar Rulz* Express packets. Pressed for time or unsure about a rule? Don't sweat it—skip it!

6. **OPTIONAL:** Write the Brain Blaster extension on your board. Ask students to work on the exercise in their notebooks or *Grammar Rulz* Express packets. The word of the day (right margin) offers additional extension for students who finish early.

7. Have your next *Grammar Rulz* exercise projected when students enter the next day.

Note: See the "Tips for Success" section for a detailed look at best practices.

Step 5—Introduce the characters!

Character 'TOONS—Anne and the Vikings

GUTHRUM	Storming in from the north, Viking bands have already defeated the Anglo-Saxon Kingdoms of Mercia and Northumbria. Now Guthrum and his ferocious Danes have set their eyes on the last remaining Anglo-Saxon stronghold—King Alfred's Wessex.	**LADY ANNE**	Anne, daughter of the powerful Earl of Kent, is savagely abducted and swept into brutal captivity. Locked in a dank, dreary dungeon at Chippenham, Anne is befriended by a handsome fellow prisoner, but can they ever escape Guthrum's clutches?
ALFRED THE GREAT	The Anglo-Saxon world is crumbling around young King Alfred's ears. Years of fighting against Viking invaders have reduced him to hiding in a swamp, but will a sudden turn of fortune snatch victory from the jaws of defeat?	**The Earl of Kent**	The Earl of Kent's only daughter, Anne, has been abducted. Saddened by his loss, the elderly earl has two options: pay an enormous ransom or forge an alliance with King Alfred to meet the Danish invaders on the field of battle.
JON	Kidnapped on the North Sea, Jon is determined to escape. While attempting to tunnel to freedom, he chances upon Anne's bleak cell. Together, they plan a bold escape scheme, but is Jon and Anne's relationship more than a mere marriage of convenience?	**GREAT BRITAIN** (Ireland)	During the Dark Ages, Britain was beleaguered by Viking attacks. At first, these Danish raiders merely plundered monasteries and vulnerable towns before returning home. Now, they're here to stay. One by one, the Anglo-Saxon kingdoms have fallen. Can anyone halt this Viking scourge?

Use *Grammar Rulz* Character 'TOONS to hook your kids on the personalities and storylines that make *Grammar Rulz* fun! Have them read the descriptions aloud and color in the characters during class or for homework. Students are likely to ask many questions: use them as a springboard to generate predictions, create connections, and activate prior knowledge. This short, relaxing activity can serve as an effective pre-reading technique that helps students "get" the story, so they can focus on the grammar.

Optional Practice Exercise

forgery (n.)

dear Tyra

I didn't never ask you to the Dance
that love note must of been a forgery
writen by my evil twin
insincerly
John

Grammar Boy sez,

End letter closings
with a little
smile—a comma.

Brain Blaster!

Write complimentary closings
from famous people:

Yours truly,   Yours forever,

Brad Pitt   _____

Warm _____   _____

_____   _____

---

forgery (n.) – a fake or counterfeit

dear Tyra,

I didn't never ask you to the Dance.
that love note must have been a forgery
written by my evil twin.
insincerely,
John

Grammar Boy sez,

End letter closings
with a little
smile—a comma.

Brain Blaster!

Write complimentary closings
from famous people:

Yours truly,   Yours forever,

Brad Pitt   _____

Warm regards,   Hugs and kisses,

_____   _____

Chapter One

The Forgotten Pharaoh

Answer keys

The Forgotten Pharaoh

Ignored by history and condemned for his father's religious beliefs, King Tutankhamen's final resting place lay forgotten for over 3,200 years. The tomb's discovery in A.D. 1922 was perhaps the most remarkable archaeological discovery of all time.

LORD CARNARVON

Poor health led dapper Lord Carnarvon to spend winters in Egypt where he discovered a passion for archaeology. After years of failure, he's investing in one final effort to locate the tomb of the forgotten pharaoh: Tutankhamen.

IBRAHIM

After working for years on the excavation of the Great Sphinx, Ibrahim is off to fabled Luxor in search of King Tut's forgotten tomb. But will he discover more than just treasure in the remote Valley of the Kings?

HOWARD CARTER

Carter, a well-known Egyptologist, scoured the Valley of the Kings for years with little success. A.D. 1922 is his last chance to make an important archaeological find before Lord Carnarvon pulls the plug on the money—and Carter's dream.

HALA

Raven-haired and mysterious, Hala doubts there is any treasure left to find in the Valley of the Kings. However, her curiosity is stirred by the sudden arrival of a handsome stranger at her father's inn.

ALI

Ibrahim's older brother will lead a team of diggers into the Valley of the Kings. Scholarly and serious, Ali dreams of one day becoming an Egyptologist and leading his own expeditions in search of Egypt's fascinating past.

Grammar Rulz!

The Nile river beggins at Africas' heart near lake Victoria. for 4241 miles, it's silt-laden current twists accross the dessert like a watery spine.

Grammar Boy sez,

Capitalize the complete names of rivers, lakes, seas, and oceans!

Brain Blaster!

List the world's longest rivers!

1. the Nile River
2. the Amazon
3. the Yangtze (Chang)
4. the Mississippi-Missouri
5. the Yenisey-Angara

My name's Ibrahim. for generations, my family, and I dwelt besides The Nile at Giza where we helped excavate The great sphinx.

Grammar Boy sez,

Where refers to location; *were* is the past tense of the verb *to be.*

Brain Blaster!

We <u>were</u> standing on the very same spot <u>where</u> they buried King Tut.

silt (n) – dirt particles in water

sphinx (n) – creature with a lion's body and a ram, human, or bird's head

In A.D. 1922, lord Carnarvon's Archaeological expedition offered higher-paying jobs to my big Brother and me, so we moved farther South to Luxor.

Grammar Boy sez,

Farther has to do with distance; further = additional.

Brain Blaster!

Seeking <u>further</u> discoveries, we plunged <u>farther</u> into the tunnel.

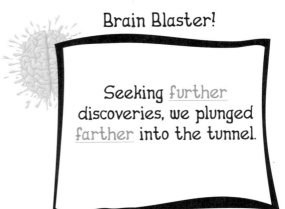

We boarded an steamer named <u>egyptian star</u> and left our old lives behind. "We have got a really enormous opportunity Ibrahim," said my brother, Ali.

Grammar Boy sez,

Underline* the names of ships, planes, and trains!

*Italicize the names when typing

Brain Blaster!

General	Specific
spaceship	<u>Apollo XIII</u>
ship	<u>Titanic</u>
train	<u>Orient Express</u>
plane	<u>Spirit of St. Louis</u>
space shuttle	<u>Discovery</u>

expedition (n) – an adventurous journey

steamer (n) – a ship powered by steam

The Forgotten Pharaoh

It was an extraordinary voyage. aggressive nile Crocodiles stalked the silty waters; venomous egyptian Cobras slithered through the reeds; and vultures hovered overhead.

Grammar Boy sez,

Use **an** before vowel sounds!

Brain Blaster!

1.	<u>An</u>	honor
2.	A	Hun
3.	An	hour
4.	An	ogre
5.	A	U-turn
6.	An	update

Ali, who's way **too** studious, was **lying** on deck reading <u>Egyptology Magazine</u> when fabled luxor came into veiw on october 21, 1922.

Grammar Boy sez,

Underline* magazine titles!

*Italicize magazine titles when typing.

Brain Blaster!

1. I read <u>Time</u>.
2. <u>Life</u> has photos.
3. <u>Mad</u> is so zany.
4. She reads <u>People</u>.
5. Let's buy <u>Seventeen</u>.

stalk (v) – to hunt stealthily

fabled (adj) – legendary or well known

archaeology (n.) – the study of ruins, artifacts

Once ashore, Ali sought out the cheif Archaeologist an englishman named Howard Carter, at Luxors winter palace hotel while I searched for lodging.

Grammar Boy sez,

Capitalize store and hotel names!

Brain Blaster!

General	Specific
supermarket	Piggly Wiggly®
gas station	Shell®
fast food	Popeye's®
convenience store	Wawa®
economy hotel	Motel 6®
luxury hotel	Ritz-Carlton®

raven (adj.) – gleaming black

As i entered a run-down inn the clerk, a beautiful raven-haired girl smiled sweetly. "A room, please," I stuttered as my cheeks reddened.

Grammar Boy sez,

"Hyphenate single-thought* modifiers before nouns!"

Brain Blaster!

Be the "HYPHENATOR"

1. Yes high-powered car
2. Yes slow-motion replay
3. Yes half-court game
4. No really cute puppy
5. No badly planned date
6. Yes big-time mistake

*Only hyphenate words that fall before (not after) the word being modified. Compare a well-known author to that author is well known. Furthermore, do not hyphenate when the first word ends in "ly": It's a truly bad movie.

"What's **your name**?"

"Hala," she answered.

"We're **here** to excavate ~~The~~ Valley ~~Of~~ The Kings," I boasted.

"There's ~~not~~ nothing left **there** to find."

Grammar Boy sez,

Break words apart to aid spelling!

Brain Blaster!

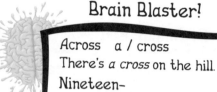

Across   a / cross
There's *a cross* on the hill.
Nineteen-
That's *nine teens* too many!
Season-
Go to *sea, son*.
Wreckage-
You're a *wreck* for your *age*!

"No, **you're** wrong," I said. "Tutankhamen's crypt wasn't ~~never~~ found."

"Who's he?"

"Tut was a teenager, Pharaoh who may **have** been assassinated 3300 years ago."

Grammar Boy sez,

Yes, set off *yes* and *no* with commas at the start of sentences!

Brain Blaster!

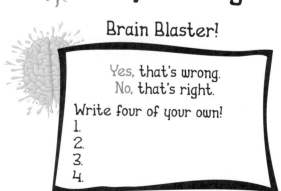

Yes, that's wrong.
No, that's right.
Write four of your own!
1.
2.
3.
4.

excavate (v.) – to dig

crypt (n.) – a burial chamber

obelisk (n.) – a pointy stone column

foreman (n.) – a supervisor of workers

After bidding Hala farewell, I admired the Ancient Egyptians' Temple Of Karnak till Ali met me between an Obelisk and a ram-headed Sphinx.

Grammar Boy sez,

Among relates three or more things; *between* relates two things.

Brain Blaster!

1. Dude, you're totally among friends.
2. Keep this between you and me.
3. The fox crept among dozens of sleeping hens.

"Mr. Carter chose me as foreman," said Ali excitedly. "You'll be my assistant." "Ali, I met this fascinating girl." "Forget her, we leaves next wednesday."

Grammar Boy sez,

Writing gains formality when you write out numbers and abbreviations!

Brain Blaster!

Make this letter very formal!

Dear Senator Hu:

Please attend Mister Lee's fifty-fifth birthday gala on Sunday.

Sincerely,

Doctor Foo

Répondez s'il vous plaît

R.S.V.P. is an acronym for the French phrase, répondez s'il vous plaît, meaning please respond.

Grammar Rulz!

Hala and I had so much in common: music, books, and even birthdays. Despite Alis' advice we spent everyday together; however, it ended too soon.

advise (v.) – to give guidance

Grammar Boy sez,

Advice (n.) = guidance; *advise* (v.) = to warn.

Brain Blaster!

I <u>advise</u> you to stop giving such lousy <u>advice</u>!

Heavy Autumn thunder boomed as a vessel carried Ali and me accross the River. we marched into the lonley, inaccessible valley of the kings.

inaccessible (adj.) – difficult to reach

Grammar Boy sez,

Avoid run-on* sentences!

Brain Blaster!

Fix this run-on in three different ways! *Tut's death mask was stuck to his face, Carter used hot knives to pry it off.*
1. ...face, and Carter...
2. ...face; Carter...
3. ...face. Carter...

*Use one of the following techniques to fix run-ons: 1) Link with a comma and a coordinating conjunction (and, but, or, for, nor, so, yet); 2) Use a semicolon, but sparingly; 3) Separate with an end mark (! or . or ?).

Name_____ Date_____ Score:_____/10 =_____%

Challenge #1

A pharaoh's burial was an enormous event. Preists spent weeks performing these steps: drying the skin, slicing open the corpse, and removing organs. Tut was then carried across the Nile river to be buried besides other Pharaohs.

On the CD, Challenge A is modified with red boxes that provide emerging learners with extra support. Challenge B has no such boxes and provides a greater challenge. When you have a moment, review the "Assessment" and "Tips for Success" sections where you'll find more ideas to help you get the most from *Grammar Rulz*.

The team assembled, at 7:00 a.m. "This season we must find Tut's tomb, or we're out of business," said Carter, a noted egyptologist, in arabic.

Grammar Boy sez,

When writing, it's helpful, I think, to set off nonessential expressions* with commas.

*I think, I believe, I wonder, on the other hand, of course

Brain Blaster!

Add nonessential expressions!

Cheeseburgers are, on the other hand, the most perfect food.

The Nile is, if I'm not mistaken, the world's longest river!

Confidence siezed Ali, and me, yet our team off fifty-five diggers was skeptical. "We never find anything," they gripped as they began shoveling rubble.

Grammar Boy sez,

Hyphenate compound numbers till you turn ninety-nine!

Brain Blaster!

Be the "HYPHENATOR"

21	twenty-one
77	seventy-seven
36	thirty-six
93	ninety-three

"Archaeology's way too hard," I whimpered. Rubbing my back, I halted as muslims do five times a day, to pray towards mecca muhammads birthplace.

Grammar Boy sez,

Capitalize religions, religious groups, and holy places!

Brain Blaster!

Religion	Group	A holy site
Islam	Muslims	Mecca
Judaism	Jews	Jerusalem
Christianity	Christians	Jerusalem

rubble (n.) – broken stone

Mecca (n.) – a holy site in Saudi Arabia

clamor (n) – a great noise or outcry

Everyday, the diggers' morale lessened but a clamor rang out one morning.
"Steps!" some one shouted.
Frantically we dug down to the twelfth step.

Grammar Boy sez,

Everyday (adj.) = ordinary; every day = each day!

Brain Blaster!

Yawn, going to school every day is such a very everyday thing.

hieroglyphics (n) – picture-based writing

A plaster wall with Hieroglyphic seals from the Ancient Egyptians' eighteenth dynasty blocked the stairway. Unfortunately there was also evidence of two tomb robbers' work.

Grammar Boy sez,

Merely add an apostrophe (twelve whales' tails) to show possession in plural nouns that end in an s.

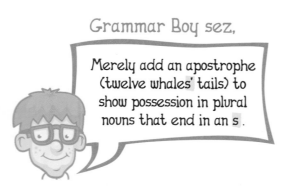

Brain Blaster!

1. These kings' crowns are cool.
2. Those surfers' boards are old.
3. Those whales' tails are huge.
4. These kids' grades are lame.
5. Those countries' cities are big.

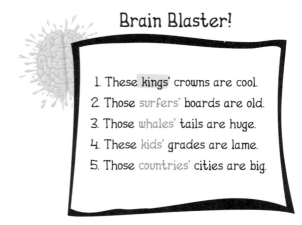

Grammar Rulz!

Unbeleivably Carter had us refill the stairway, before scuttling off to telegraph London.

Weeks later lord carnarvon and his daughter the lovely lady Evelyn arrived.

Grammar Boy sez,

Hey, use commas to set off introductory words.

Brain Blaster!

1. Stumbling, he fell forward.
2. Nonetheless,
3. Well,
4. Panting,
5. Panicking,

When we resummed excavation, Tut's name soon became legible. alot of the diggers' shovels lead us onwards toward another sealed entry. the fatefull moment had arrived.

Grammar Boy sez,

You have apostrophe options* when singular nouns (Athens, James) end with an s.

*It's standard practice to add an extra 's to possessive singular nouns ending in s when (James's car) they are easy to say; however, some writers omit the second s when (Ares' axe) the addition of a second s makes for awkward pronunciation.

Brain Blaster!

If it's easy to say...
Otis's iPhone
James's book

However, if it's hard to say...
Xerxes' attack
Socrates' speech
Ulysses' voyage
Arkansas' governor
Ramses' crown

scuttle (v.) – to run in choppy steps

legible (adj.) – possible to read or interpret

chariot (n) – a horse-drawn war cart

shrine (n) – an altar or place of worship

Carefully, we clambered into a Royal Tomb that had **lain** quiet for 3,200 years. Carter's candle illuminated war chariots, treasure chests and gaurdian statues.

Grammar Boy sez,

The mighty q is almost always followed by u.

Brain Blaster!

Use a dictionary to find out where the few exceptions come from!

Qatar (Arab nation)
Qoph (Hebrew letter)

Beyond another door **lay** four Golden shrines. they were gaurded by winged isis, and covered with magic spells from the <u>Book Of The Dead</u>.

Grammar Boy sez,

Underline* book titles!

*Italicize book titles when typing.

Brain Blaster!

Write about your favorite books!
1. <u>Holes</u> is a really original book.
2.
3.
4.
5.

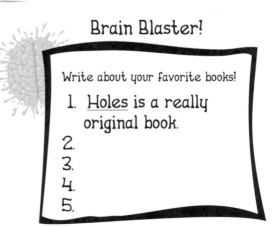

A sarcophagus holding coffins was lying inside the fourth Shrine. The final coffin had been beaten from 250 pounds of pure Gold. Tut's Mummy lay within.

Grammar Boy sez,

To lie = to recline;
to lay = to place.

It's confusing because the past tense of *to lie* is *lay.*

Brain Blaster!

To lie
I'll lie down tonight.
I lay down last night.*
I was lying down.
He'd have lain there forever.

To lay
I'll lay bricks today.
I laid bricks yesterday.
I was laying bricks.
I had laid the bricks yesterday.

Nineteen-years-old Tut lay hidden beneath a gold death mask. priests had pulled his brain through his nostrils and embalmed his Liver and Lungs.

Grammar Boy sez,

Hyphenate ages that fall before nouns* till you become a ninety-nine-year-old person.

*Don't hyphenate when a single-thought adjective cluster falls after the noun or pronoun. Compare a *two-year-old boy* to the boy *is two years old.*

Brain Blaster!

Hyphenate!

1. twelve-year-old rock star
2. one-year-old monster
3. He's ten years old.
4. sixteen-year-old singer
5. They're fifteen years old.

pundit (n) – a writer who offers opinions

Yes we'd realized our Goal. Pundits says no undiscovered Tombs remains. Nevertheless, as I gaze out over the shifting, egyptian sands, I know they're wrong.

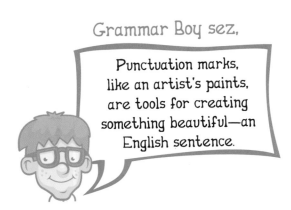

Grammar Boy sez,

Punctuation marks, like an artist's paints, are tools for creating something beautiful—an English sentence.

Brain Blaster!

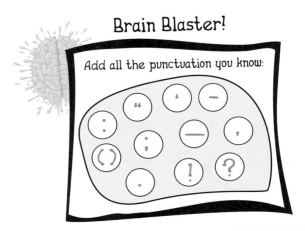

Add all the punctuation you know:

Name_____ Date_____ Score:_____ /10 =_____ %

Challenge #2

Sadly, lord Carnarvon died five months later, and the news lead alot of people to believe in a curse. Nevertheless, Ali and I felt fine after working everyday in the tomb for twenty-four months. Fortunately, I found my own treasure when I proposed to Hala.

On the CD, Challenge A is modified with red boxes that provide emerging learners with extra support. Challenge B has no such boxes and provides a greater challenge. When you have a moment, review the "Assessment" and "Tips for Success" sections where you'll find more ideas to help you get the most from *Grammar Rulz*.

Chapter Two

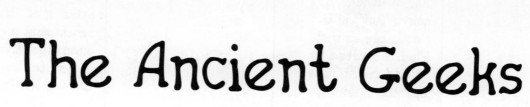

The Ancient Geeks

Answer keys

Character 'TOONS—The Ancient Geeks

Aphrodite, the totally gorgeous goddess of love, is always there to provide hot-headed Zeus with a bit of clever advice. Born from the sea, she's famed for her charming allure, but will Aphrodite's wit and beauty be enough to save Athens from the wrath of a seriously grumpy Zeus?

APHRODITE

Armed with a bow and a quiver full of love-inducing arrows, Aphrodite's naughty son, Eros, is always stirring up trouble. Known to the Romans as Cupid, his amorous arrows cause their unsuspecting targets to fall madly in love with the first person they see—often with disastrous effects.

EROS

Hermes, the wing-footed messenger of the gods, spends most of his time snoozing on Mount Olympus. Suddenly, Zeus sends him to discover why the Athenians are making such a racket on the Acropolis. Hermes whisks off, but can our ever-forgetful hero even manage to find Athens?

HERMES

A rattling, clattering racket awakens mighty Zeus from his gentle slumber near the summit of Mount Olympus. Flying into a towering rage, he's close to destroying Athens with a well-aimed thunderbolt when Aphrodite, the goddess of love, suggests a more subtle course of action.

ZEUS

Phidias, though a mere mortal, is an artist among artists. His extraordinary statues are part of what makes the Golden Age of Athens so... golden. But will the masterpieces that Phidias created be able to withstand a Spartan onslaught in the impending Peloponnesian War?

PHIDIAS

Pericles isn't just another mortal: he's done much to strengthen Athenian democracy during his decades in power. Yet in spite of the splendor of Athens, resentment is growing among the other Greek city-states: war is brewing. Will Pericles be able to guide Athens safely through this, his greatest challenge?

PERICLES

A commotion woke zeus on the hieght of mount Olympus. his stern eyes swept over the mountainous greek countryside and came to rest on athens.

Grammar Boy sez,

Capitalize the names of gods and deities.

Brain Blaster!

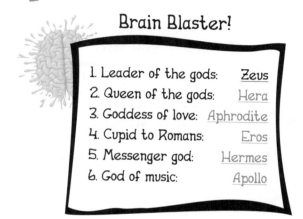

1. Leader of the gods: Zeus
2. Queen of the gods: Hera
3. Goddess of love: Aphrodite
4. Cupid to Romans: Eros
5. Messenger god: Hermes
6. God of music: Apollo

"Ugh, it's saturday morning, and they're hammering away on thier stupid acropolis over there," zeus muttered into his mammoth white beard.

Grammar Boy sez,

*There = yonder;
they're = they are;
their shows ownership.*

Brain Blaster!

They're worried

their old car won't make it there.

stern (adj.) – serious, businesslike

acropolis (n.) – a high place in a Greek city-state

lethal (adj.) – way deadly

"I'll **teach those** numbskulls a lesson!" cried Zeus. he was aiming a lethal thunderbolt at the parthenon when a lovley goddess appeared besides him.

Grammar Boy sez,

Capitalize building names.

Brain Blaster!

List some cool buildings!
1. the Parthenon
2. the Sears Tower
3. the White House
4. the Freedom Tower
5. the Louvre

lustrous (adj.) – glossy, silky

"Zeus, **they're** building Tempals in all of the olympians honor" purred Aphrodite, the goddess of love, as her lustrous hair glittered in the Sun.

Grammar Boy sez,

Dude, set off names and nicknames in direct address.

Brain Blaster!

Use *dude* at the beginning, middle, and end of a sentence.
Dude, that's my taco.
1. Dude, stop the insanity.
2. Stop the insanity, dude.
3. It's time, dude, to stop the insanity.

"Well, ill spare athens if The Parthenon's beautiful."

"But Hera won't never let you out off her sight," said Aphrodite.

"Let's send Hermes to investigate."

Grammar Boy sez,

Site (n.) = a location; *sight* (v.) = to notice or observe.

Brain Blaster!

Use both words in a single sentence!

Captain Lee was the first to sight the enemy missile site.

As ussual, Mt. Olympus's wing-footed courier was snoozing. Eros interrupted Hermes's beautiful nap, and they **flew** quickly to Zeus's side.

Grammar Boy sez,

Singular nouns show possession with an apostrophe and an s (Joe's car, James's pup) unless hard to say:

Usually-Zeus's beard
Sometimes-Ares' ax.

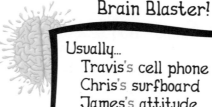

Brain Blaster!

Usually...
    Travis's cell phone
    Chris's surfboard
    James's attitude
But sometimes...
    Ares' sword
    Sophocles' play
    Achilles' fate

spare (v.) – to show mercy

courier (n.) – a messenger

After recieving Zeus's orders Hermes flewed South along the Balkan penninsula towards Athens but his sandals where on the wrong feet. He veered off course.

Grammar Boy sez,

Only capitalize directions in specific place names like South America.

Brain Blaster!

Write three sentences using uppercase and lowercase directions.

Let's go south to South Africa!

1.
2.
3.

Raceing through a Spring storm Hermes niether stopped nor slept. he was flying more lower to avoid lightning when a polis came into sight.

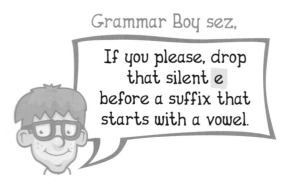

Grammar Boy sez,

If you please, drop that silent e before a suffix that starts with a vowel.

Brain Blaster!

1. hope + ing = hoping
2. hope + ful = hopeful
3. hope + less = hopeless
4. use + ful = useful
5. use + ing = using
6. use + less = useless

veer (v.) – to suddenly turn

polis (n.) – ancient Greek word for a self-governing city-state

In the feilds teenager soldiers where exercising with razor-tipped pikes, thick, sturdy shields and short iron swords.

"Rats its sparta," groaned Hermes. "How depressing."

Grammar Boy sez,

Well, set off a mild interjection with a comma.

Brain Blaster!

Write sentences that begin with mild interjections. Dang, I'm good.

1.
2.
3.

Suddenly martial cries and the clash of spears on sheilds rang out. lines of soldiers snapped to attention while king Archidamus II came into veiw.

Grammar Boy sez,

Capitalize titles before names.

Brain Blaster!

List some famous (or infamous) royalty.

1. King Midas
2. Emperor Nero
3. Czar Nicholas II
4. Emperor Napoleon
5. Queen Elizabeth I

pike (n) – a long, heavy spear

martial (adj) – related to war

spartan (adj.) — basic, serious

"Spartans!" Archidamus cried. "For too long those athenian losers have built their Empire, but this Spring our army will break Athens' power."

Grammar Boy sez,

Brake (v.) = to slow;
break (v.) = to crack;
break (n.) = a rest.

Brain Blaster!

Hoping our car's brakes wouldn't <u>break</u>, we <u>braked</u> slowly and then took a <u>break</u>.

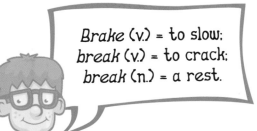

---

haughty (adj.) — proud, scornful

"I can't hardly believe it," Said Hermes. "Things might have been different if those greeks' attitudes weren't so haughty. Boy, I need advice."

Grammar Boy sez,

Use *might have* in place of *might of*.

Brain Blaster!

Might of =   Might have
Could of =
Should of =
Would of =
May of =
Never of =

Grammar Rulz!

Filled with worry, Hermes shot straight Northwards towards the oracle at delphi where a preistess foretold the future at the temple of apollo.

Grammar Boy sez,

For clarity, consider setting off introductory material with a comma*.

*At times writers choose to omit a comma after a short prepositional phrase, but always use a comma when clarity demands it.

Brain Blaster!

1. In the east, New York came into view.
2. Slowly, Zoe's vision returned.
3. After returning the money, Larisa felt better.

oracle (n.) – a wise person thought to foretell the future

Name_____ Date_____ Score:_____/10 =_____%

Challenge #1

Well, those proud, artistic Athenians and those hostile Spartans where ready to fight. Athens' plan was to use its powerful fleet. Sparta's plan was to send it's well-trained soldiers North.

On the hieght of Mount Olympus, the Olympians faces showed their displeasure.

On the CD, Challenge A is modified with red boxes that provide emerging learners with extra support. Challenge B has no such boxes and provides a greater challenge. When you have a moment, review the "Assessment" and "Tips for Success" sections where you'll find more ideas to help you get the most from *Grammar Rulz!*

chasm (n.) – a deep, narrow opening

audible (adj.) – capable of being heard

Disguising **himself** as Mortal, Hermes, he entered the Temple where an hideous, toothless sorceress sat wreathed in fumes raising from a wierd chasm.

Grammar Boy sez,

Rise (v.) = to get up; *raise* (v.) = to lift up.

Brain Blaster!

After <u>rising</u>, Joe yawned and <u>raised</u> the blinds.

"Oh powerful! Oracle, War is gathering. What's **going to** happen?"

"Twenty-seven winters will pass before the Owl **dies**," came the priestess' barely audible murmur.

Grammar Boy sez,

Don't capitalize* the seasons.

Brain Blaster!

Write a single sentence that mentions the four seasons.

*Seasons are sometimes capitalized when personified.
Example: *Finally, Spring's balmy breath melted the snow.*

Hermes' pondered the cryptic message. After an hour his sandals led him to the athenian countryside where Athens lay shinning like a gem in the Spring sun.

Grammar Boy sez,

Capitalize proper adjectives.

Brain Blaster!

Change these nouns to proper adjectives:

Mexico = Mexican flag
England = English policy
Brazil = Brazilian ship
Andes = Andean nation
Patagonia = Patagonian ax
Paris = Parisian bistro

Hermes landed in an agora where Goats, wine, and olives were sold. forty-one macedonian slaves lay huddled together as merchants haggled over their prices.

Grammar Boy sez,

To lie = to recline; *to lay* = to place.

Brain Blaster!

To lie
I'll lie down now.
I lay down last night.
I am lying down.
He'd have lain there forever.

To lay
I'll lay bricks now.
I laid bricks yesterday.
I am laying bricks.
I had laid the bricks yesterday.

cryptic (adj.) – having secret meaning

haggle (v.) – to argue over prices

ascent (n.) – a steep climb

Hermes's ascent to The Acropolis was really steep. Standing among eight columns of shining Marble, the world-renowned sculptor Phidias examined his achievements with patience.

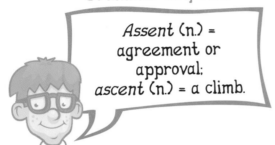

Grammar Boy sez,

Assent (n.) = agreement or approval; ascent (n.) = a climb.

Brain Blaster!

After gaining China's _assent_, she began her perilous _ascent_ of Mt. Everest.

faze (v.) – to bother or perturb

"Greetings Phidias," Cried Hermes. "I've already heard alot about The Parthenon. I'm dyeing to hear whether this phase of building is going well."

Grammar Boy sez,

Good is usually an adjective; well is usually an adverb!

Brain Blaster!

Insert good or well:

1. I swam _well_!
2. He's a _good_ dog!
3. Run _well_ today!

Grammar Rulz!

"You and **I** should see Athena's statue. it's thirty-three feet in hieght, covered in Ivory, and gilded in 2000 pounds of Gold leaf," said Phidias.

Grammar Boy sez,

Cover the extra pronoun to avoid confusion!

Brain Blaster!

1. You and I rock.
2. He and she will win.
3. Pay her and me.
4. He and we are mad.
5. Donate it to him and them.

gild (v) – to coat with gold

"Now, however, it maybe time for Pericles' speech," said Phidias.

They descended the Parthenon's West gradient where 6000 Citizens, the Ecclesia, awaited their leader.

Grammar Boy sez,

Set off parenthetical expressions with commas.

Brain Blaster!

1. It is, I think, bogus.
2. I can, therefore, do it.
3. That is, I believe, mistaken.
4. It is, however, bad karma.
5. I did, nonetheless, eat cake.

gradient (n.) – a slope

There weren't no slaves, women, or foriegners. Silence fell as Pericles's speech began. "Countrymen, i've recieved dispatches from Sparta that I can't hardly believe."

dispatch (n.) – a message or news

Grammar Boy sez,

Capitalize specific place names!

Brain Blaster!

General	Specific
river	Rhine River
sea	Coral Sea
bay	Bay of Bengal
island	Angel Island
desert	Negev Desert

"Those nasty spartans have made unacceptable demands, it's War! We'll relinquish Attica, defend Athens, and attack by Sea," said Pericles, showing his well-known calm.

relinquish (v.) – to give up something

Grammar Boy sez,

Hyphenate single-thought adjectives!

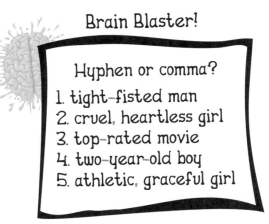

Brain Blaster!

Hyphen or comma?
1. tight-fisted man
2. cruel, heartless girl
3. top-rated movie
4. two-year-old boy
5. athletic, graceful girl

The Ancient Geeks

"You and I must part, Phidias," Said Hermes. "Maybe there's time to stop the Peloponnesian war!" He cried while rocketing torwards the twelve olympians home.

Grammar Boy sez,

Capitalize specific historical events.

Brain Blaster!

List some world-shaking events:
1 the Russian Revolution
2. the Renaissance
3. the Black Death
4. the Battle of Britain
5. the Harlem Renaissance
6. the Industrial Revolution

The Gods waited on mt. olympus. "Tell me Hermes what's occurring down there?" asked Aphrodite. "Yeah, I should have already annihilated Athens!" bellowed Zeus.

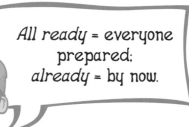

Grammar Boy sez,

All ready = everyone prepared; already = by now.

Brain Blaster!

I already asked if the pizzas were all ready.

hostilities (n) – conflict or fighting

bellow (v) – to shout or roar

altruism (n) – selfless caring for others

transform (v) – to change or modify

"No need for your thunderbolts Zeus. They're all ready too obliterate themselves. All their altruism is destroyed by pride, greed and aggression. won't Humanity never change?"

Grammar Boy sez,

Grammar is a tool, like a sculptor's chisel, that helps us create beauty.

Brain Blaster!

List the eight parts of speech:

Prepositions
Adjectives
Pronouns
Adverbs
Verbs
Interjections
Nouns
Conjunctions

"Only one thing can transform those violent Mortals," Aphrodite whispered.

"What's that?" asked Zeus, and Hermes.

"Why its love you fools. loves their only hope."

Grammar Boy sez,

Ancient Greece lives on in the English language!

Brain Blaster!

Find the origins of these words:

history, idiot, microscope, method, arctic, hieroglyph

Name_____ Date_____ Score:_____ /10 =_____ %

Challenge #2

Twenty-seven years passed, but the Peloponnesian War eventually lead to Athens defeat. The athenian soldiers fought well, but Pericles and alot of others died in a terrible plague. the city's power was broken, and the Golden Age of Athens came to an end.

On the CD, Challenge A is modified with red boxes that provide emerging learners with extra support. Challenge B has no such boxes and provides a greater challenge. When you have a moment, review the "Assessment" and "Tips for Success" sections where you'll find more ideas to help you get the most from *Grammar Rulz*.

Chapter Three

Trouble at Vesuvius
Answer keys

Character 'TOONS—Trouble at Vesuvius

Marcus

M.M.

The son of a Roman architect, Marcus lives in the beautiful town of Pompeii. He's fascinated by the sights and sounds of this bustling Roman city, particularly the gladiators who draw him to Pompeii's amphitheater on a fateful August morning in A.D. 79.

Lucia

M.M.

Lucia is wealthy and free, but she's a slave to fashion. She's usually falling in and out of love with the latest cute gladiators or shopping at the forum, but the sudden eruption of Mount Vesuvius thrusts Lucia into a position of leadership. Does she have what it takes to rescue her family?

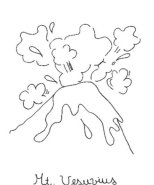

Mt. Vesuvius

M.M.

From the streets of Pompeii, Mount Vesuvius appears to be little more than a peaceful mountain. Little do the citizens of Pompeii know, for deep beneath the mountain's green-clad slopes, a sea of molten magma lies ready to explode!

Demitrios

M.M.

The family tutor, Demitrios, comes from Greece. Like so many Roman tutors, he is a slave. Despite his encyclopedic knowledge of Greek literature, Lucia and Marcus are less than fond of their tutor. Will they ever be able to rely on him when tragedy strikes Pompeii?

Julia

M.M.

A Syrian slave such as Julia could expect little from life, yet the family's cook fills Marcus and Lucia's home with light and laughter. Despite her lowly social status as a kitchen slave, Julia makes the very best of each day, and Lucia and Marcus simply adore her.

Rufus

M.M.

As a puppy, Rufus was given to Marcus as his tenth birthday present, and since then they've become like brothers. When disaster strikes, the two become separated on the ash-choked streets of Pompeii. Will Rufus ever see his young master again?

Grammar
Rulz!

My name is Marcus Secundus. a month has **passed** since the Cataclysm yet I still can't hardly believe what's happened. this is my story.

Grammar Boy sez,

Don't write no double negatives!

Brain Blaster!

I can't hardly walk.
It isn't anywhere.
I can't scarcely breathe.
There isn't anybody home.
He will never go.
I haven't never seen it.

My Family and I lived in beautifull Pompeii on the bay of naples. my Father, an architect, was repairing damage from the 62 A.D. earthquake.

Grammar Boy sez,

A.D. is Latin for *Anno Domini** and is best placed before a year.

Brain Blaster!

A.D. = *Anno Domini*
B.C. = Before Christ
C.E. = Common Era
B.C.E. = Before the Common Era

A.D. 79 or 79 C.E.
100 B.C. or 100 B.C.E.

*A.D. = *Anno Domini* (year of our Lord in Latin): B.C. = Before Christ:
C.E. = Common Era: B.C.E. = Before the Common Era. Some scholars choose to use B.C.E. and C.E. because they are nonreligious terms.
You choose!

Because off father's privileged position, I could go anywheres; however, I was drawn like a Moth to flame by the amphitheater and it's feirce gladiators.

Grammar Boy sez,

It's = it is; *its* shows possession.

Brain Blaster!

Use both words in a sentence!
1. Gross, it's cleaning its ears!
2. Its fur stinks. It's so disgusting!
3. It's time to charge its battery!

On a Summer day, my bossy sister, Lucia, took me to see Gladiators training, they where from! alot of places; Greece, Africa, and even Gaul.

Grammar Boy sez,

Colons only introduce lists after a part of a sentence* that can stand alone.

*An independent or main clause

Brain Blaster!

Use a colon in a sentence!

It was the perfect meal: chili dogs, corn bread, and warm chocolate chip cookies.

Write your own!

amphitheater (n.) – a stadium

Gaul (n.) – ancient name for France

Trouble at Vesuvius

"That's Claudius with the Trident," sighed Lucia.

"You're in love again," I laughed. "What's happened to Quintus?"

Lucia pouted, and pointed her thumb downwards.

Grammar Boy sez,

Latin is the mother of today's modern Romance languages!

Brain Blaster!

List some Romance languages you'd like to learn!

1. Spanish
2. Portuguese
3. Italian
4. Catalan
5. Romanian
6. French

Twenty-two Gladiators were fighting practice bouts with wooden weapons. training was going well when a tremor shook the Earth.

"Oh, no!" I shrieked.

Grammar Boy sez,

Good is usually an adjective; *well* is usually an adverb.

Brain Blaster!

1. I have a <u>good</u> job, and it pays <u>well</u>.
2. He writes <u>well</u>; he's a <u>good</u> author.
3. I have <u>good</u> friends who treat me really <u>well</u>.

trident (n) – a three-pointed spear

bout (n) – a match or contest

Grammar Rulz!

Trouble at Vesuvius

extinct (adj.) – no longer active or living

"Calm down Marcus. You're too jumpy," said Lucia.

"Those tremors comes from mt. vesuvius," I said.

"That's impossible, it's an extinct volcano, dummy."

Grammar Boy sez,

Capitalize specific geographic features.

Brain Blaster!

Plan a road trip! We'll make five stops on our coast-to-coast road trip: the Grand Canyon, the _____, the _____, the _____, and even the _____.

magma (n.) – molten rock underground

Noone knew that a Sea of high-temperature Magma lay bellow Vesuvius verdant slopes. Enormous pressure built up as it sought to break loose.

Grammar Boy sez,

Loose (adj.) = not tight; *lose* (v.) = the opposite of *to win* or *to find*.

Brain Blaster!

1. I hope I don't lose my loose tooth tonight.

2. Our loose wheel made us lose the race!

3. I never lose dollar bills or loose change!

Grammar
Rulz!

Walking home, we marveled at prosperous Pompeii. there were bathes, theatres, and fountains; furthermore, there were businesses, an amphitheater, an aqueduct, a forum, and Temples.

Grammar Boy sez,

Capitalize proper nouns. Don't capitalize common nouns.

Brain Blaster!

Sort into two columns!

augustus, emperor, colosseum, stadium, hun, barbarian, war, punic war, queen, cleopatra

Common	Proper
emperor	Augustus

Near our villa, I bought loaves of bread, and Lucia, who couldn't never resist jewelry, spent a whole Silver denarius on an Ivory hairpin.

Grammar Boy sez,

Use commas, which are punctuation marks, to set off nonessential stuff.

Brain Blaster!

Add nonessential expressions!

1. Pizza, which is a great food, is often round.
2. New York, which is also called the Big Apple, looks good in snow!
3. Joe, who bugs me a little, is very funny.

forum (n.) – a public square in ancient Rome

villa (n.) – a spacious and luxurious Roman residence

chide (v.) – to scold

"You're late!" our syrian cook chided.

"Sorry, Julia," I grinned. "Hey, why's Rufus barking?"

"Your Hound's wierd, Marcus. Now, go lie down for lunch."

Grammar Boy sez,

The past tense of *lie* (to recline) is *lay*. The past tense of *lay* (to place) is *laid*.

Brain Blaster!

1. Spot, go <u>lie</u> down!
2. Earlier, I <u>lay</u> down.
3. Now, go <u>lay</u> bricks!
4. Earlier, I <u>laid</u> bricks!

odyssey (n.) – a quest or search

After lunch, our tutor, a knowledgeable athenian slave named Demetrios, shouted, "Lessons should have already started! We have got to beggin mathematics, and Homer's <u>Odyssey</u>."

Grammar Boy sez,

Use mnemonics (memory tricks) to improve your spelling.

Brain Blaster!

How will you remember these words?

Knowledge – You have to know where the ledge is!
Misspell – Miss Pell
Attendance – At ten [we] dance
Dessert – Strawberry shortcake for dessert

Grammar Rulz!

Name_____ Date_____ Score:_____ /10 = _____%

Challenge #1

The beautiful? Colosseum,* a roman stadium, was built in 79 A.D. by Emperor Titus, and his Father. Gladiators who fought well in the arena where sometimes set free .

*Note: Colosseum is spelled correctly.

On the CD, Challenge A is modified with red boxes that provide emerging learners with extra support. Challenge B has no such boxes and provides a greater challenge. When you have a moment, review the "Assessment" and "Tips for Success" sections where you'll find more ideas to help you get the most from *Grammar Rulz.*

Hopeing to avoid another whipping, we gathered scrolls, and wax writting tablets. Suddenly, an ear-shattering boom tore through the air, and shook the Earth.

Grammar Boy sez,

Don't overuse commas!

Brain Blaster!

1. The ball is blue, and red.
2. Let's wait, and see.
3. They hop, skip, and jump.
4. They'll drool, or slobber.
5. He's neither tough, nor fair.

scroll (n.) — a rolled length of paper

We desperately hurried into via Fortuna. Farther North an enormous colunm of smoke rose from Vesuvius. darkness fell as ash, and loose pumice rained down.

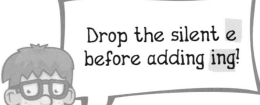

Grammar Boy sez,

Drop the silent e before adding ing!

Brain Blaster!

Hope + ful = hopeful
Hope + less = hopeless
Hope + ing = hoping
Use + ful = useful
Use + less = useless
Use + ing = using

We retreated to safety.

"Let's wait for father," Said Lucia. "Julia collect valuables. Marcus gather cushions."

"Why?"

"To sheild your empty skull you dolt."

Grammar Boy sez,

Capitalize family titles if they can be replaced by a name.

Brain Blaster!

1. Thanks, Mom.
2. She's my sister.
3. Let's ask Dad.
4. My aunt's mean.
5. That's Uncle Moe.

Grammar Rulz!

After an hour, Father wasn't nowheres to be seen.

"He should have been here, where is he?" asked Lucia.

"He's repairing The Temple Of Venus."

Grammar Boy sez,

> Capitalize centers of religious worship.

Brain Blaster!

> List famous temples, churches, synagogues, or mosques:
> 1. the Blue Mosque*
> 2. the Pantheon
> 3. Notre Dame
> 4. Chartres Cathedral
> 5. Angkor Watt
> 6. Luxor Temple
>
> * In Istanbul, Turkey

Let's us go," I recommended.

Julia, Demetrios, Lucia, and I staggered onwards through knee-deep ash, as piteous cries from lost children cut through the blackness.

Grammar Boy sez,

> Remember tricky spellings with memory tricks.

Brain Blaster!

> How will you remember these words?
>
> Earring – Dude, think twice before putting that ring through your ear!
> Carrot – My car [will] rot!
> Forward – It's for Ward.
> Across – There's a cross.

Venus (n.) – Roman goddess of love

piteous (adj.) – causing pity; sad

shrine (n) – an altar or place of worship

Near venus' Shrine, I tripped on something.

"Ouch," Said a familiar voice.

"Father!"

"Marcus, I'm badly hurt, and don't know whether I can walk."

Grammar Boy sez,

The *weather* (n.) is forecast on TV: *whether* (conj.) = if.

Brain Blaster!

I wonder *whether* the *weather* will get better.

progeny (n) – children or offspring

"Father, let's carry you to our boat, Fortuna, which lies on the river."

"I can't ~~scarcely~~ believe it's my own progeny who are rescuing me."

Grammar Boy sez,

Use *which* to refer to things; use *who* to refer to people.

Brain Blaster!

1. They are the ones who love pizza.
2. Which of these pizzas tastes better?

We proceeded South. Hot, venomous ash affected us; nevertheless, we reached the River, and we boarded the boat.
Suddenly, panic coursed through my viens.

Grammar Boy sez,

Run away from run-on* sentences!

Brain Blaster!

Fix this run-on in three different ways!

Mt. Vesuvius erupted like an atomic bomb, Pompeii was doomed.

1. ... bomb, and Pompeii...
2. ... bomb; Pompeii...
3. ... bomb. Pompeii...

*Use one of the following techniques to fix run-ons: 1) Link with a comma and a coordinating conjunction (and, but, or, for, nor, so, yet); 2) Use a semicolon, but sparingly; 3) Separate with an end mark (! or . or ?).

course (v) - to flow swiftly

"We forgot Rufus!" I shrejked.
"If I'm not back in an hour, leave without me," Said Lucia's steady, unruffled voice as she left.

Grammar Boy sez,

Two modifiers before a noun can be left alone, split with a comma, or joined with a hyphen*.

Brain Blaster!

a. two old books-	nada
b. happy, joyful song-	comma
c. well-loved book-	hyphen
d. picture-perfect pizza	hyphen
e. hot July day	nada
f. several smelly dogs	nada
g. warm summer night	nada
h. clever, intelligent boy	comma
i. light-fingered thief	hyphen

* Don't hyphenate if the first word is an adverb. ending in ly as in "rapidly melting ice," etc.

unruffled (adj.) - cool as a cucumber

gnash (v.) – to grind together

callous (adj.) – unfeeling

Julia wept as the hours passed. Noone could breathe well, and Lava lit the night like Vulcans vengeance. Father lay unconscious, and Demetrios teeth gnashed.

Grammar Boy sez,

Nobody is, you know, like, kind of informal; *no one*, however, is rather formal.

Brain Blaster!

Sort 'em!
Somebody, someone, anyone, anybody, everyone, everybody

Formal:	Informal:
No one	Nobody
someone	somebody
anyone	anybody
everyone	everybody

"Let's leave. Lucia's probably had an accident or died," Said Demetrios callously.

"Never," said I.

Demetrios rose to full height, and siezed a paddle.

Grammar Boy sez,

Dye (v.) = to color; *die* (v.) = to stop living.

Brain Blaster!

1. Dye that shirt!
2. My goldfish died!
3. I'm dying of thirst!
4. Quit dyeing your hair!
5. Cool tie-dyed shirt!

Grammar Rulz!

Ignoreing my arguéments, he began paddling. I was powerless, but Julia lunged out off the gloom, and sent Demetrios tumbling into the inkey water.

Grammar Boy sez,

Don't get sinked, I mean sunk, by irregular verbs!

Brain Blaster!

Present tense	Past tense
catch	caught
lead	led
creep	crept
swing	swung
choose	chose
seek	sought

"Never trust anybody whose Brain is stronger than his Heart," Julia chortled.

Then we heared barking as Lucia splashed forwards with Rufus over her shoulders.

Grammar Boy sez,

Mighty Rome lives on in the English language!

Brain Blaster!

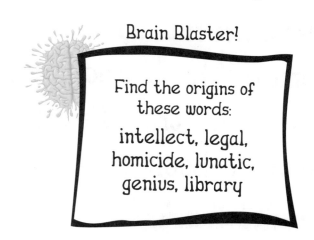

Find the origins of these words:

intellect, legal, homicide, lunatic, genius, library

lunge (v) – to leap forward

chortle (n.) – combination of a chuckle and snort

He and she who were completely exhausted and grimey clambered into the boat.

"Lucia that was so incredibly … "

"Shut up and row Marcus," she grinned.

Grammar Boy sez,

Rome lives on in our calendar and solar system!

Brain Blaster!

What do these Roman words give us?

Rome's war god –	planet Mars
Rome's goddess of love –	planet Venus
Rome's messenger god –	planet Mercury
Julius and Augustus –	July and August
Roman number 10 (decem) –	December
Roman number 9 (novem) –	November
Roman number 8 (octo) –	October

Name_____ Date_____ Score:_____/10 =_____%

Challenge #2

Pompeii lay buried and forgotten for 1,600 years. Rufus lived a long, and happy life with his master, Marcus who studied in roman schools and became a senator. Lucia moved farther North to Rome where she wrote a book called <u>Trouble at Vesuvius</u>.

On the CD, Challenge A is modified with red boxes that provide emerging learners with extra support. Challenge B has no such boxes and provides a greater challenge. When you have a moment, review the "Assessment" and "Tips for Success" sections where you'll find more ideas to help you get the most from *Grammar Rulz*.

Chapter Four

Anne and the Vikings

Answer keys

Character 'TOONS—Anne and the Vikings

GUTHRUM

Storming in from the north, Viking bands have already defeated the Anglo-Saxon Kingdoms of Mercia and Northumbria. Now Guthrum and his ferocious Danes have set their eyes on the last remaining Anglo-Saxon stronghold—King Alfred's Wessex.

LADY ANNE

Anne, daughter of the powerful Earl of Kent, is savagely abducted and swept into brutal captivity. Locked in a dank, dreary dungeon at Chippenham, Anne is befriended by a handsome fellow prisoner, but can they ever escape Guthrum's clutches?

ALFRED THE GREAT

The Anglo-Saxon world is crumbling around young King Alfred's ears. Years of fighting against Viking invaders have reduced him to hiding in a swamp, but will a sudden turn of fortune snatch victory from the jaws of defeat?

The Earl of Kent

The Earl of Kent's only daughter, Anne, has been abducted. Saddened by his loss, the elderly earl has two options: pay an enormous ransom or forge an alliance with King Alfred to meet the Danish invaders on the field of battle.

JON

Kidnapped on the North Sea, Jon is determined to escape. While attempting to tunnel to freedom, he chances upon Anne's bleak cell. Together, they plan a bold escape scheme, but is Jon and Anne's relationship more than a mere marriage of convenience?

Ireland

GREAT BRITAIN

During the Dark Ages, Britain was beleaguered by Viking attacks. At first, these Danish raiders merely plundered monasteries and vulnerable towns before returning home. Now, they're here to stay. One by one, the Anglo-Saxon kingdoms have fallen. Can anyone halt this Viking scourge?

Grammar Rulz!

A Winter Sun rose slowly over the frigid english fields. bells jingled as lady Anne's eight Horses pulled her sleigh along an icy track.

Grammar Boy sez,

I before E except after C or when it sounds like the aaay in Santa's sleigh.

Brain Blaster!

List some aaay exceptions:
1. Their
2. vein
3. reign
4. eighth
5. foreign

frigid (adj.) — seriously cold

Anne's thoughts where interrupted by the twang of a bowstring, and an arrow whistling past. Swiftly, twenty-one feirce vikings surrounded the sleigh.

Grammar Boy sez,

Than makes a comparison; then concerns time.

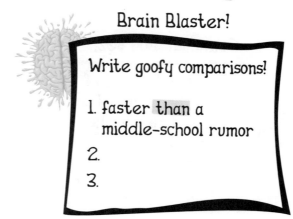

Brain Blaster!

Write goofy comparisons!

1. faster than a middle-school rumor
2.
3.

twang (n) — a vibrating sound

Grammar Rulz!

marauder (n.) – a raider or plunderer

Anne could go niether forwards nor backwards. she dropped the riens, and pulled two daggers as the circle of axe-wielding marauders drew more closer.

Grammar Boy sez,

For a stylish sound*, try forward in place of forwards.

*Style is, of course, a choice. *Forwards* (adv.) is an informal version of *forward*. Consider dropping the "s" in formal situations.

Brain Blaster!

Consider** the difference!

anyway (adv.) vs. anyways
anywhere (adv.) vs. anywheres
nowhere (adv.) vs. nowheres
somewhere (adv.) vs. somewheres

**The difference, of course, has to do with formality. *Anyways* is a less formal version of *anyway*. Some sources hold that *anywheres, nowheres,* and *somewheres* aren't words, yet we hear them in everyday speech. The trick is to modulate your level of language based on the formality of the situation.

Norseman (n.) – man of the north, Viking

Like a Cat, Anne struck at the most nearest norseman; nonetheless, he seized her wrists, and twisted them cruelly till the knives dropped.

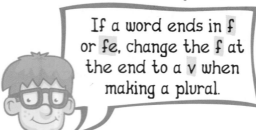

Grammar Boy sez,

If a word ends in **f** or **fe**, change the f at the end to a **v** when making a plural.

Brain Blaster!

knife becomes knives
wife becomes wives...
life becomes lives
leaf becomes leaves
elf becomes elves
thief becomes thieves
shelf becomes shelves

"What's youre name, poppet?" Guthrum demanded as he raised Anne's chin with an axe. His pale eyes had an really wierd effect on her.

Grammar Boy sez,

Effect is usually a noun; *affect* is usually a verb.

An effect (n.) = a result or impact; to affect (v.) = to influence

Brain Blaster!

That movie's special <u>effects</u> totally <u>affected</u> the crowd.

"You filthy foriegners have no right to hear my name," Anne scoffed.

Guthrum grabbed her lunch bag. "Well, this says lady Anne Of Kent," he chuckled.

Grammar Boy sez,

Rite (n.) = a ceremony; *right* (n.) = a privilege.

Brain Blaster!

The law guaranteed Joey and Zoe's legal <u>right</u> to join hands together in the <u>rite</u> of marriage.

poppet (n.) – a term of endearment used like "sweetie" or "honey"

scoff (v.) – to laugh or snort rudely

ransom (n.) – payment to return a hostage

mutton (n.) – roasted sheep flesh

"Rats moms still writting my name on my lunch bag," said Anne.

"You're going to fetch alot of ransom," Guthrum snarled.

"My Dad wont dessert me!"

Grammar Boy sez,

A lot is two words, but it's best to avoid* this vague expression.

*Except in dialogue

Brain Blaster!

Rescue this sentence with numerical detail:

A dozen murderous Vikings swarmed aboard our boat.

"You'll bring a hefty ransom, or loose your head poppet," Guthrum snarlled. his teeth were shattered stumps, and his breathe reeked off rotted mutton.

Grammar Boy sez,

To breathe (v.) = to inhale; *breath (n.) =* respiration.

Brain Blaster!

Dude, I can't <u>breathe</u> 'cause your <u>breath</u> reeks.

Grammar Rulz!

The rogues lead Anne straight too a sleek, longboat named <u>Hammer Of Thor</u>. it was lying parallel to the banks of The Thames river.

Grammar Boy sez,

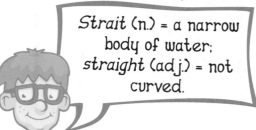

Strait (n.) = a narrow body of water; *straight* (adj.) = not curved.

Brain Blaster!

Sketch a straight strait:

rogue (n.) – a scoundrel or bad guy

Anne's ransom letter arrived February 3, 878.

Daddy,

I've been siezed by Vikings who demands 10000 Silver pennies to set me loose.

Yours in peril,

Anne :(

Grammar Boy sez,

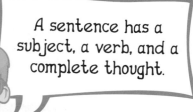

A sentence has a subject, a verb, and a complete thought.

Brain Blaster!

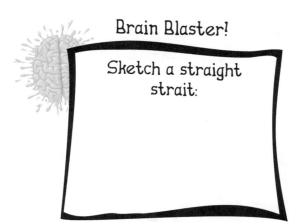

Circle the subject and underline the verb:
1. (Bears) <u>eat</u> honey.
2. (Bees) sting bears.
3. A (boy) <u>meets</u> a girl.
4. A (girl) <u>meets</u> a boy.

peril (n.) – serious danger

Grammar Rulz!

Wednesday, February 4, 878 A.D.

Anne,
Your ransom will be paid. Stay hopefull untill then, and wait for further instructions.
love,
Dad

Grammar Boy sez,

Drop the second L when adding the suffix full to form an adjective*.

*But adverbs such as *powerfully* and *beautifully* take a second L

Brain Blaster!

Power+full = powerful
Beauty+full = beautiful
Fret+full = fretful
Fruit+full = fruitful
Watch+full = watchful
Use+full = useful
Fit+full = fitful

"Steward!" cried the earl Of Kent. "Send this by messenger. Meanwhile, I'll ride West to wessex too seek aide from king Alfred the great."

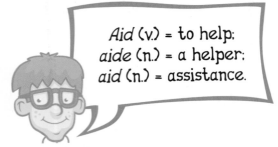

Grammar Boy sez,

Aid (v.) = to help;
aide (n.) = a helper;
aid (n.) = assistance.

Brain Blaster!

That young teacher's <u>aide</u> gave us <u>aid</u> with math. She worked hard to <u>aid</u> us.

Back in Viking-controlled Chippenham, Anne was separated from everyone, imprisoned in a dreary, dark cell, and getting really desperate.

Grammar Boy sez,

Everyone = the whole bunch;
every one = each individual.

Brain Blaster!

Everyone must keep listening to every one of my mushy love songs.

dreary (adj.) – sad and gloomy

Without warning, stones bursted out off the wall. Anne laid down her writing quill, lay on the floor, and peered into the murky whole.

Grammar Boy sez,

To lie (v.) = to recline
Now, I lie down.
I lay down last night.

To lay (v.) = to place
Now, I lay bricks.
I laid bricks yesterday.

Brain Blaster!

Present tense
Go lie down to sleep.
Lay down the book.

Past tense
I lay down to sleep.
I laid down the book.

quill (n.) – feather used for writing

Anne and the Vikings

abduct (v) – to kidnap or take by force

"Whose there?" gasped Anne.

"The name's Jon," said a strong adolescent voice. "I've been here since dad and I where abducted by those danes."

Grammar Boy sez,

Thursday comes from Thorsdagr, Old Norse for Thor's day!

Brain Blaster!

Sunday comes from ... the Sun's day

Monday come from ... the Moon's day

Wednesday comes from ... Woden's (father of the Anglo-Saxon gods) day

Name_____ Date_____ Score:____/10 =____%

Challenge #1

Vikings with wierd names like Eric Bloodaxe and Thorfinn Skullsplitter lead alot of separate attacks on Europe. everyone despaired as the fierce Norsemen drew more closer, but Alfred the great rose up and saved England from further conquest.

On the CD, Challenge A is modified with red boxes that provide emerging learners with extra support. Challenge B has no such boxes and provides a greater challenge. When you have a moment, review the "Assessment" and "Tips for Success" sections where you'll find more ideas to help you get the most from *Grammar Rulz*.

Anne and the Vikings

"Hush! Some one's coming," Anne whispered urgently. "Whew, now he's gone. You and I can talk now, Jon."

"Let's pass notes instead," murmured Jon.

Grammar Boy sez,

Oh, don't forget to set off mild interjections with a comma.

Brain Blaster!

Use 'em: *aw, rats, hah, ugh, pshaw, yikes, doh, jeepers*

Aw, that's cute.

_____ , _____

_____ , _____

_____ , _____

_____ , _____

Dear Anne,

    You're voice fills dad and me with resolve. we have to break out soon.

yours truely,

Jon ;)

P.S. How old are you?

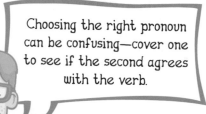

Grammar Boy sez,

Choosing the right pronoun can be confusing—cover one to see if the second agrees with the verb.

Brain Blaster!

1. He and I like gum.
2. That's from her and me.
3. He and she argued.

murmur (v) – talking in a low voice

resolve (n) – a firm choice or decision to do something

Dear Jon,

Yes, let's escape. I can't hardly wait to meet you.
Till Tonight,
Anne :)
P.S. My sixteenth birthdays on wednesday, february 28, 878.

Grammar Boy sez,

There's no need to add endings like th and st to numerical dates.

Brain Blaster!

Write proper dates for your birthday and Independence Day:
July 21, 1965
or
21 July 1965

At 4:30 a.m. Jon and his Dad wriggled in to Anne's cell.

"Let's do this," said Jon as he hided.

"Help guard help!" Anne screamed loudly.

Grammar Boy sez,

Adverbs can describe verbs and often end in ly.

Brain Blaster!

List some ly adverbs:
walk stealthily
think quickly
dance gracefully
drive defensively
play joyfully

Grammar Rulz!

two norsemen peered through the grate, and saw Anne lying on the straw. As they hurried in, Jon knocked the two hapless guards heads together.

Grammar Boy sez,

Lying can mean fibbing or reclining.

Brain Blaster!

He was totally <u>lying</u> about <u>lying</u> down to sleep.

Useing the two guards keys, the trio fleed the dungeon. the prison courtyard was desserted; the portcullis was open; and there weren't no Vikings anywheres.

Grammar Boy sez,

Never write no double negatives!

Brain Blaster!

1. can hardly see
2. it's not nowhere
3. can scarcely breathe
4. not never going

hapless (adj.) – unlucky, unfortunate

portcullis (n.) – a castle gate

lance (n.) – a long spear

Suddenly, horns blared, horses nieghed, and lances clashed. Outside, two armies faced eachother.

"It's Alfred the great!" cried Anne. "He and dad are finally here."

Grammar Boy sez,

Capitalize epithets like Erik the Red.

Brain Blaster!

List historical figures who earned an epithet:

Peter the Great
Cyrus the Great
Ivan the Terrible
Lorenzo the Magnificent

Now, invent epithets for everyone in your family! Be nice!

hasten (v.) – to rush or hurry

On Alfred's command, english archers launched clouds off arrows that blocked the Sun; nevertheless, the Vikings sheltered under their round sheilds and then hastened forward.

Grammar Boy sez,

Semicolons and conjunctive adverbs can link two sentences; however, try not to overuse them.

Brain Blaster!

Conjunctive Adverbs

furthermore, consequently
nevertheless, therefore

Link two sentences with a semicolon and a conjunctive adverb followed by a comma.

I seldom use the semicolon; even so, there are times when it seems to fit perfectly.

Grammar Rulz!

The Vikings fought truely well but they where no match for Alfreds troops. As the Viking's retreated , Anne and Jon ventured onto the battlefeild.

Grammar Boy sez,

Use *good* to modify nouns and pronouns; use *well* to modify verbs.

Brain Blaster!

I played _well_ and threw some _good_ passes.

She made some _good_ shots and dribbled _well_.

Anne's dad rode towards Anne, but Guthrum was fiegning death. he leaped* up, knocked Anne down, and held an axe to Jon's Jugular vien.

*Or leapt

Grammar Boy sez,

Banish run-on** sentences!

Brain Blaster!

Fix this run-on in 3 different ways! Ivar the Boneless was a Viking leader, he terrorized England.

1. ...leader, and he...
2. ...leader; he...
3. ...leader. He...

**Use one of the following techniques to fix run-ons: 1) Link with a comma and a coordinating conjunction (*and, but, or, for, nor, so, yet*); 2) Use a semicolon, but sparingly; 3) Separate with an end mark (! or . or ?).

venture (v.) – to attempt something dangerous or difficult

feign (v.) – to pretend or fake

"Try any thing wierd and i'll..."
Suddenly a really well-thrown dagger skewered Guthrums hand. Shreiking he fleed. Anne had saved the day.

Grammar Boy sez,

Use *real* as an adjective; use *really* as an adverb.

Brain Blaster!

1. Your bling is <u>really</u> lame.
2. I'm <u>really</u> tired.
3. That's a <u>really</u> ugly dog.
4. Dude, that's a <u>real</u> shark.
5. Her car is <u>really</u> slow.

"Jon helped me flee from captivity, Father," Anne said as her Dad embraced her.

"kneel," commanded the earl of Kent. "I knight thee sir Jon."

Grammar Boy sez,

Capitalize family titles used in direct address.

Brain Blaster!

Write some dialogue using uppercase family titles at the end of the sentence:

1. "Thanks for the BMW, Mom!"
2. "What's the dealio, Pop?"
3.
4.

skewer (v.) – to pierce completely

captivity (n.) – a period spent in jail

Anne smiled, took Jon's arm, and kissed his cheek.

Jon blushed, grabbed an arabian stallion's mane, and leapt a top. "Let's us go," he said.

Grammar Boy sez,

There are often several ways to say or spell a word in English—choice is good.

Brain Blaster!

1. leaped or	leapt
2. burnt or	burned
3. axe or	ax
4. fish (plural) or	fishes
5. learned or	learnt
6. gray or	grey
7. Ta may toe (pronunciation) or...	toe ma toh

Anne accepted Jon's hand, and swung up besides him. An light snow began drifting downward as he and she cantered away too the Southeast.*

Grammar Boy sez,

Don't capitalize directions unless they're part of a place name.

Brain Blaster!

1. Walk six paces west.
2. Head northeast to West Virginia.
3. Go south to South Carolina!
4. I want to live in the South.

*Capitalize regional names like the *South* or the *Northwest*, but don't capitalize cardinal or intermediate directions.

stallion (n.) – a male horse

canter (v.) – to run at a medium pace

Before he and she disappeared from sight, the unmistakeable sound off Anne's laugh floated across the frozen feilds like a hint of Spring.

Grammar Boy sez,

The Vikings are alive in our language today.

Brain Blaster!

Find out where these words came from:
leg, egg, sky, anger, cake, steak

Name_____ Date_____ Score:____ /10 =____ %

Challenge #2

Anne and Jon shared many truely exciting adventures before she and he arrived at Kent Castle. As the years passed, their love grew, and Anne accepted Jon's marriage proposal. The wedding went well. They where quite happy, yet vikings dominated much of the english countryside for years to come.

On the CD, Challenge A is modified with red boxes that provide emerging learners with extra support. Challenge B has no such boxes and provides a greater challenge. When you have a moment, review the "Assessment" and "Tips for Success" sections where you'll find more ideas to help you get the most from *Grammar Rulz*.

Resources

Grammar Notes

A comprehensive discussion of grammar could run to hundreds of pages—a level of detail that certainly lies beyond the scope of this section. What seem to be required here are a few observations on how to address a variety of troublesome conventions and some thoughts on how to build a solid conventions program that will keep students learning and growing throughout the year.

It's worth noting at the onset that English has no handlers, no masters. Spain and France have their academies—ancient corps of language gatekeepers enthroned at Madrid and Paris—that delineate and produce official dictionaries; English, on the other hand, cheerfully throws up its hands and recognizes usage as its ultimate authority. The result, of course, is utter chaos for students as they wade through alternate spellings—*travelling* vs. *traveling*—varied verb conjugations—*sank* vs. *sunk*—and inexplicable rules of punctuation and capitalization. Yes, it's bedlam, but teachers can seize on each inconsistency and champion it as an opportunity for students to choose, to decide, to take ownership. Teachers can use every glitch, every exception as a chance to frame English for what it is: a language that's too vibrant, too rich, and too alive to be pinned to the mat and defined into submission.

Before delving into minutiae, it should also be mentioned that a teacher's general perspective on language can significantly impact student learning; indeed, it can be fairly argued that a flexible, non-prescriptive attitude may serve to better engage students in making knowledgeable, creative decisions about writing and speaking. Moreover, offering informed choices rather than prescribing any right or wrong way to use English aptly mirrors the delightful diversity of our language and our world.

Punctuation

Students tend to view punctuation with a mixture of fascination and puzzlement—and although many are keen to decode the baffling dots, curls, and ciphers that swirl across their writing, merely naming them remains a challenge for most. Consequently, labeling may be a logical first step for teachers. Posting Punctuation Nation placards (printable versions can be found on the CD) provides students with a handy visual reference for use throughout the school year. If you want to enlarge these posters past the 11 x 17-inch size your copy center can offer, consider seeing your tech specialist for instructions on how to print posters on multiple sheets of paper that students cut and tape together.

English punctuation offers a great deal of flexibility. When a point of optional punctuation arises, encourage students to make an informed choice rather than dictating a correct way to do it. *Grammar Rulz* reflects this broadminded perspective by placing dotted proofreading marks in areas of optional punctuation.

Semicolons

Use a semicolon to join two related independent clauses into a compound sentence; bear in mind, however, that this device ought to be used quite sparingly.

Use a semicolon before conjunctive adverbs such as *moreover, furthermore, nevertheless, nonetheless, therefore*, etc., to link two related independent clauses into a compound sentence. *I don't like my job very much; therefore, I think that I'm going to quit.*

Use a semicolon to separate items in a series that are themselves divided by commas. *We visited Paris, France; Madrid, Spain; Moscow, Russia; and, best of all, Camden, New Jersey.*

Colons

Use a colon to introduce a list of items that follows an independent clause. *This year I visited four countries: Brazil, Argentina, Mexico, and Zimbabwe.*

Use a colon to act as a pointer that adds a dramatic pause before what follows. It's sort of like a joke and the punch line. *There's a problem with your joke: it's not funny.*

There seems to be little agreement about capitalizing the first word of an independent clause that follows a colon. Common guidance includes capitalizing direct quotations and sentences that want emphasis when they follow a colon. Here again, consider the old shibboleth: be consistent throughout.

Hyphens

Use hyphen(s) to join *single-thought* adjectives as well as adverbs that don't end in *ly*.

Use hyphen(s) to link compound words such as *commander-in-chief*.

Use hyphens to link compound numbers from *twenty-one* to *ninety-nine*.

Commas

Use a comma to separate words, phrases, or clauses in a series. The last comma in the series (that which often precedes a coordinating conjunction) is optional but recommended when clarity is gained through its use. Consider the following sentences:

Go buy me a hoagie, ham, and cheese.

Go buy me a hoagie, ham and cheese.

Without a second comma, the reader might be forgiven for thinking you just want a big ham and cheese hoagie instead of a hoagie *and* ham *and* cheese. Lunch might be ruined—all on account of that missing comma.

Use a comma to separate equal adjectives. *She's a graceful, charming girl.*

Generally, use a comma to set off introductory words, phrases, and clauses. *At times* writers choose to omit the comma after short prepositional phrases. It's sometimes helpful to point out that writing gets more flexible in creative genres such as poetry, drama, screenplays, fiction, etc.

Set off names in direct address, Igor.

Igor, set off names in direct address.

You know, Igor, you should set off names in direct address.

Set off parenthetical information, *also known as extra stuff,* with commas.

Set off non-essential expressions, *which can be removed without changing the essential meaning of the sentence,* with commas.

Yes, set off *yes* and *no* with commas when those words appear at the start of a sentence.

Apostrophes

Use an apostrophe to show possession. Singular nouns that end in an "s" are a problem area. Experts show enormous inconsistency on this point: some hold that adding an apostrophe and an "s" is required though contemporary writers seem to be leaning in quite the opposite direction. If you'd like to find a comfortable middle ground, consider the following sensible guideline: singular nouns show possession by adding an apostrophe and an "s" unless they're awkward to say. Thus, it's usually *Zeus's* beard but sometimes *Ares'* ax.

Plural nouns that end in "s" show possession by merely adding an apostrophe. *Yikes! I really have to find the boys' room.*

Dashes

Dashes come in three tasty flavors, and they're lurking inside the INSERT > SYMBOLS > SPECIAL CHARACTERS option on the Microsoft Word® toolbar.

1) The figure dash is often used between groups of digits in a telephone number. *609-667-9294*

2) The en dash is the width of a capital "N" and can mean *until* or *to. OPEN 9–5* or the *Paris–Dakar Rally.*

3) The em dash is the width of a capital letter "M" and can be used in pairs in the manner of parentheses or singly in the manner of a colon. One straightforward use of the em dash is to set off non-sequential or random breaks in the flow or direction of a sentence. *I've always wanted to visit Prague—though I'm not quite sure where it is—in the fall.*

Work with letters! Letters are a punctuation-intensive form of writing. When you can, cast writing assignments in the form of letters to help students master some of the trickier conventions presented in this mode of communication that remains, despite our digital age, a peerless form.

Proofreading marks are a vital shorthand that students will use constantly in the decade or so that passes between entering sixth grade and graduation from college. Although there are many variants, *Grammar Rulz* provides a basic set of symbols that teachers and students can use to communicate about writing. Have students copy or paste these SUPER PROOFER proofreading symbols into their notebooks at the start of a unit or the year. These symbols can be found on the CD and page xx. If you want to enlarge the SUPER PROOFER poster past the 11 x 17-inch size your copy center can offer, consider seeing your tech specialist for instructions on how to print posters on multiple sheets of paper that students can cut and tape together to form mega-posters.

Grammar Rulz provides important daily practice in basic punctuation that can and should be augmented by teaching punctuation in context, consistent feedback on written work, and continual reteaching of problem areas.

Spelling

The disorderly nature of English spelling is a byproduct of the rich history of our tongue. Despite Noah Webster's semi-successful attempts at taming the language's orthographic quirks, English spelling stubbornly retains a rather amusing eccentricity. At first blush, teaching spelling can seem an overwhelming task, but a logical initial step is to offer a brief history of English. A *lively* historical overview can give students a sense of the diverse origins of what some commentators estimate to be a 500,000-

word vocabulary. When the opportunity arises, present notoriously thorny English spelling as a trade-off for a vast vocabulary that makes writing in English so much fun. This immense lexicon is a feast: encourage students to celebrate its extensive range and colorful word origins. Most of all, the 500,000-words-in-English statistic may stir up a bit of curiosity about language history, may shine a sliver of light on etymology, and may open a discussion about how words are created. Not bad for a factoid!

Four Useful Rules

It's i before e except after c or when it sounds like the aay in Santa's sleigh.

believe, receive, their, eight, weight, vein, heir

If you please, drop the silent e before a suffix that starts with a vowel.

like > liking > likeness; hope > hoping > hopeless

The mighty q is usually followed by u.

quiet, quit, quick

When words end in f or fe, change the f at the end to a v when making a plural.

calf becomes calves; wife becomes wives; life becomes lives

There are other spelling rules, but many teachers doubt the benefit (at least at the middle-school level) of learning and applying these somewhat arcane guidelines. As an alternative, consider addressing spelling through some of the programmatic practices discussed below.

Dictionaries, though fundamental resources, often receive scant attention. Ideally, students have easy access to dictionaries throughout their school day, but in reality this is rarely the case. Think about that for a moment. We demand that students spell correctly, yet the very tool needed to build their spelling sits twenty feet away on a dusty shelf. Students are left with two lousy options: lay bare their ignorance by raising a hand for teacher assistance (something poor spellers rarely do) or guess—most choose the latter. To help students spell, some teachers place a dictionary atop every student's desk. Others plant a small research library (dictionary, thesaurus, atlas, etc.) in the basket under student chairs. In the unlikely case that piles of money are available, consider purchasing desktop electronic dictionaries (one for every pair of students) that can create a welcome spike in spell checking. If you're working in a wealthy district, encourage families to purchase personal electronic dictionaries.

On a programmatic note, dictionaries often become misallocated and spread out over the years. Organize a school-wide dictionary hunt, and you'll be amazed at the sheer number of books you uncover. Re-assemble and redistribute dictionaries in grade-level sets. Whenever your language arts department is up for textbook adoption, don't forget to use it as an opportunity to update or augment dictionary sets.

On a tech note, make use of software and the Internet. Choose a reliable online dictionary that you'd like students to use. Another solid move is teaching your students how to properly use the Spelling/Grammar feature of Microsoft Word.

Common Middle-School Misspellings:

A lot	Exhausted	Outrageous
Absence	Furniture	Parallel
Accidentally	Extremely	Particularly
Accurate	Excitement	Peculiar
Achievement	February	Peninsula
Acquire	Finally	Perceive
Aisle	Foreign	Piece
Appropriate	Forgetful	Pleasant
Approval	Forty	Possession
Assessment	Fourth	Potatoes
Athletic	Frustrating	Powerful
Attention	Genius	Privilege
Author	Governor	Professor
Audience	Government	Professional
Awesome	Grammar	Realize
Balloon	Guarantee	Receipt
Beautiful	Height	Restaurant
Beginning	Imagine	Responsible
Believe	Immediately	Rhythm
Boredom	Independent	Safety
Business	Interesting	Scenery
Calendar	Interrupt	Science
Category	Invader	Sense
Cemetery	Island	Sentence
Character	Jealousy	Separate
Chief	Knowledge	Servant
Chaos	Length	Sincerely
Chronological	License	Simile
Colonel	Likely	Skiing
Column	Loneliness	Solely
Comfortable	Lovely	Speech
Completely	Manageable	Successful
Conjunction	Marriage	Succeed
Conscience	Mediterranean	Surprise
Consecutive	Message	Surrender
Controlled	Metaphor	Surround
Criticize	Miniature	Temperature
Criticism	Mischievous	Tension
Definitely	Misspell	Through
Decision	Mysterious	Thorough
Defense	Naturally	Tomorrow
Disappoint	Neighbor	Tournament
Disease	Ninety	Truly
Disastrous	Nineteen	Unnecessary
Dissatisfied	Necessary	Unmistakable
Effectively	Obstacle	Useful
Emphasize	Occasion	Usually
Envelope	Occasionally	Violence
Environment	Onomatopoeia	Wednesday
Excess	Opinion	Weird
Excellent	Opportunity	Whether

Morphology (the study of word formation) has long been a building block of vocabulary instruction, but the morphological examination of base words, root words, prefixes, and suffixes can also be a powerful spelling tool. Take the word *earring*, for example. Noticing that this is a combination of two base words, *ear* and *ring*, helps students avoid misspelling this word. On a similar note, simple spelling rules like "If you please, drop the silent 'e' before a suffix that starts with a vowel" can help students master suffix-related spelling problems. Finally, help students become aware of word formation techniques such as blended (breakfast + lunch = *brunch*) words, person (scientist Franz Mesmer's name forms the base word of *mesmerize*) words, and shortened (memo is short for *memorandum*) words that can add a helpful level of understanding.

Syllabification (breaking words into syllables) is another effective spelling technique. Anything difficult—be it a scientific phenomenon or a tricky spelling word—can be simplified by breaking it down into its basic parts. Make syllabification a basic part of all your vocabulary work!

Mnemonics (memory tricks) are powerful tools that help students master difficult spelling words. Troublesome words such as *attendance* are easily learned by breaking words into memory-activating chunks like *at ten* [we] *dance*. Other tricky spelling words such as *dessert* can be memorized with phrases such as *the best dessert is strawberry shortcake*, a reference to the double "s" in *dessert*.

Individualize your spelling program! The My Spelling Gremlins individualized spelling sheet—found on page 89, located on the CD, and embedded in each *Grammar Rulz* Express packet—integrates the methods (basic morphology, mnemonics, syllabification, etc.) discussed previously. Have students paste copies of My Spelling Gremlins into their notebooks. Use it, or any similar method, to individualize your spelling program. Whenever reviewing student tests or writing, merely highlight any misspellings and ask students to analyze them.

Alternate spellings and regional variants pepper our language with variety and richness. Though famed American lexicographer Noah Webster led partially successful efforts at spelling reform in the nineteenth century, English remains replete with alternate spellings; in fact, some of his well-intentioned reforms seem to have further complicated the language, at least from an international perspective. Young writers frequently encounter choices such as *burned* or *burnt*, *learned* or *learnt*, *theater* or *theatre*, *ax* or *axe*, *color* or *colour*, *traveled* or *travelled*, *realized* or *realised* and *gray* or *grey*. It's probably best to encourage students to prefer the primary dictionary spellings (standard spellings are listed first) while, as always, framing any discussion around choices. Then again, there seems to be very little harm in allowing students to prefer *grey* over *gray*; indeed, one could argue that a student who makes that sort of informed choice is beginning to take ownership of language, and that, my friends, is huge! Furthermore, when students know the stories behind these options—international variants, mixed usage, Webster's spelling reforms—they gain context and clarity that, in the end, will help to improve their spelling.

Online resources are a powerful ally. The Internet is packed with excellent spelling games and quizzes that can serve as valuable extension exercises. In addition, many textbooks offer online companion exercises. Students will find these online resources to be interesting, and most teachers will appreciate the learning potential of these highly interactive resources.

Grammar Rulz provides important daily practice in basic spelling that can and should be augmented by teaching spelling in context, providing consistent feedback on written work, and continually reteaching problem areas.

Capitalization

In Hebrew, there are no capital letters. Seriously. In German, you capitalize every noun. Seriously. In Spanish, capitalization is light and sensible.

English, by contrast, forces its writers to navigate a murky capitalization netherworld, lost somewhere between the buoyant common sense of Spanish and heavy-handed *über* capitalization.

For most students, English capitalization remains a labyrinth of custom and tradition that largely defies rational explanation. Perhaps more than any other writing convention, proper capitalization requires memorizing a litany of rules. *Grammar Rulz* certainly addresses the important concepts (proper vs. common nouns) and rules that underpin English capitalization; in addition, it attempts to shine a slice of light on the study of word origins, etymology, which can sometimes be useful when students ask that best of questions, "Why do I have to capitalize this?" In the case of days or months or planets, an exploration of word origins can add an element of logic to what often seems—capitalize the months but not the seasons, for example—a poorly mixed cocktail of rules. Below, please find a smattering of rules.

Capitalize holidays:
1. Groundhog Day
2. New Year's Day
3. April Fools' Day

Capitalize family titles used in direct address:
Thanks, *Dad*, for being a good *dad*.

Capitalize *epithets*:
1. Erik *the Red*
2. Ivar *the Boneless*
3. Ivan *the Terrible*

Don't capitalize directions unless they're part of a place name:
1. Walk six paces west.
2. Head north to West Virginia.
3. Go south to South Carolina!
4. I want to live in the South.

Capitalize the names of gods and deities:
Zeus, Hera, Aphrodite, etc.

Capitalize building names:
1. the Parthenon
2. the Empire State Building
3. the World Trade Center

Capitalize titles before names:
1. King Midas
2. Queen Elizabeth
3. Emperor Hirohito

Don't capitalize the seasons:
winter, spring, summer, fall, autumn

Capitalize proper adjectives:
1. *Mexican* flag
2. *Russian* caviar
3. *Japanese* food
4. *Italian* boyfriend

Capitalize specific historical events:
1. the Russian Revolution
2. the Iron Age
3. the Italian Renaissance

Capitalize specific geographic features:
1. the Grand Canyon
2. the Columbia River
3. Mount Olympus

Capitalize proper nouns:
1. Augustus
2. Hun
3. Punic War

Don't capitalize common nouns:
1. an emperor
2. a barbarian
3. a war

Capitalize centers of religious worship:
1. the Blue Mosque
2. the Vatican
3. the Wailing Wall

Capitalize store and hotel names:
1. Piggly Wiggly® (supermarket)
2. Ritz-Carlton Hotel®

Capitalize religions, prophets, religious groups, holy places, and holy books:
1. Hinduism
2. Buddha
3. Christians
4. Mecca
5. the Koran

Capitalize specific school names:
1. Oxford University
2. University of Oregon

Capitalize languages—all 6,000 of them:
1. Mandarin Chinese
2. Swahili
3. Romanian

Capitalize brand names:
1. Reebok®
2. Kellog's®

Only capitalize the first word in a complimentary closing:
1. Best regards,
2. Sincerely yours,
3. Yours truly,

Capitalize specific course titles:
1. Advanced Skateboarding 301
2. Effective Flirting 101

Capitalize organizations:
1. Red Cross
2. United Nations

Common nouns and proper nouns are, of course, the logical place to start. Grammar texts offer useful exercises, and concept formation in this area is critical enough to warrant continual focus and repetition.

Grammar Rulz provides all-important daily practice in basic capitalization that can and should be augmented by teaching capitalization in context, providing consistent feedback on written work, and continually reteaching problem areas.

Usage

A young Oklahoman once assured me that the word "anywhere" didn't exist; his point was perfectly logical because "anywheres" was what family and friends said. After listening, I agreed that "anywheres" was the perfect word for him to use with his buds, and he, after checking a dictionary, agreed that dropping the "s" *might* be better if—and only if—he was giving a Heisman Trophy acceptance speech. For this student, the rich vernacular of his hometown was more relevant than *The Chicago Manual of Style*.

Similar situations occur when discussing double negatives. People use them all the time, and when you think about it, a well-placed double negative—"Yo, I'm not lending you no more money!"—can be just what you need if you're hanging tough on a South Philly street corner. Likewise, "I guess what I be sayin' is that I wanna get to know you a little better…" might be your smoothest move in another zip code. President Obama can serve nicely as a summative example. The language he chooses when shooting hoop with friends in Chicago is quite different than the language he chooses when addressing Congress.

Dialect, vernacular, idiom, local usage, and regional accents all add richness to our language—and what a loss it is when we attempt to smother everything non-standard. Teachers should always seek to broaden rather than homogenize language, so it may be best to respect the sometimes rough-cut language of our students while always searching for ways to help them develop a more standard English they can call upon when the situation requires. One way to put this issue to bed is writing a bit of dialogue in the third person. Students who resist using formal English often enjoy this exercise because it lets them use authentic language from the street, yet the dialogue tags, action sequences, and descriptions tend to be a more standard English. It's very disarming for students to see, on the same page, language used at varying levels of formality; it lets them see that their vernacular isn't some pidgin abomination—and that is a bridge to a more open discussion of language.

Advice (n.) = guidance; *advise* (v.) = to warn

Aid (v.) = to help; *aide* (n.) = a helper; *aid* (n.) = assistance

All ready = everyone prepared; *already* (adv.) = by now

Among (prep.) relates three or more things; *between* (prep.) relates two things

Assent (n.) = agreement or approval; *ascent* (n) = a climb

Brake (v.) = to slow down; *break* (v.) = to crack; *break* (n.) = a rest

Breathe (v.) = to inhale; *breath* (n.) = respiration

Dye (v.) = to color; *die* (v.) = to stop living

Effect = a change or impression or occurrence and is usually a noun; *affect* = to influence and is usually a verb

Everyday (adj.) = ordinary; *every day* = each day

Everyone (pron.) = the whole bunch; *every one* = each individual

Farther has to do with distance; *further* = additional

It's = it is; *its* shows possession

Lie (v.) = to recline; *lay (v.)* = to place

Lie
I'll *lie* down tonight.
I *lay* down last night.
I am *lying* down.
He would have *lain* there forever.

Lay

I'll *lay* bricks today.

I *laid* bricks yesterday.

I am *laying* bricks.

I would have *laid* the bricks yesterday.

Loose (adj.) = not tight; *lose* (v.) = the opposite of *to win* or *to find*

Real is an adjective; *really* is an adverb.

Rise (v.) = to get up; *raise* (v.) = to lift up

Rite (n.) = a ceremony; *right* (n.) = a privilege

Site (n.) = a location; *sight* (n.) = something noticed or observed

Strait (n.) = a narrow body of water; *straight* (adj.) = not curved

Than (conj.) makes a comparison; *then* (adv.) concerns time

There = yonder; *they're* = they are; *their* shows ownership

Weather (n.) is forecast on TV; *whether* (conj.) = if

What's = *what is* or *what has*

Where refers to location; *were* is the past tense of the verb *to be*

Grammar

Simply put, grammar is a set of shared ideas about how words and sentences are formed. Grammar helps us communicate complex ideas in crisp, elegant prose that informs, persuades, entertains, and enriches others.

The good news is that your students already know grammar. Prove it to them by writing this sentence on the board: *Wants my brother to be a doctor witch.* Now, ask them to fix it without adding any new words. With luck, most will recast the sentence in one of two equally upsetting but grammatically happier versions: *My brother wants to be a witch doctor* or *A witch doctor wants to be my brother.* Without being able to say it, most students know that the subject in the original sentence (*brother*) normally precedes the verb (*wants*), and they know that an adjective generally precedes the noun it modifies. This is grammar. If there arises an unlikely clamor for further examples, have students use dictionaries to add as many prefixes and suffixes as humanly possible to a base word: *human*. When they've finished the exercise, tell students that the way words are formed is also part of grammar.

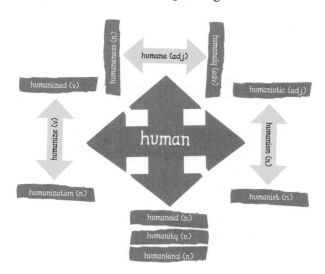

In spite of academic efforts to hold grammar down and define it into submission, the term remains a useful everyday catchword for writing conventions (spelling, capitalization, punctuation, grammar, and usage) as a whole. It's interesting to note that this common-sense colloquial usage matches reality in the sense that the conventions of writing (particularly punctuation and grammar) often overlap and interact.

Good is usually an adjective; *well* is usually an adverb.

A sentence has a subject, a verb, and a complete thought.

Choosing the right pronoun can be confusing— cover one to see if the second agrees with the verb.

1. You and ~~me~~ rock!

Correction: You and I rock!

2. ~~Him~~ and she will win.

Correction: He and she will win.

3. Pay ~~she~~ and ~~I~~?

Correction: Pay her and me.

4. ~~Him~~ and ~~us~~ are mad.

Correction: He and we are mad.

5. Donate it to ~~he~~ and them.

Correction: Donate it to him and them.

Never write ~~no~~ double negatives!

Semicolons and conjunctive adverbs can link two independent clauses; however, try to be careful not to overuse them.

Independent clauses can be married together by a semicolon; this acts to form a compound sentence.

Avoid run-on sentences! Use one of the following techniques to fix run-ons: 1) Link with a comma and a coordinating conjunction (*and, but, or, for, nor, so, yet*); 2) Use a semicolon, but sparingly; 3) Separate with an end mark. If students remark that they sometimes see run-on sentences in fiction, respond with this old zinger: *you only get to use them when you're famous.*

Grammar Rulz provides all-important daily practice in basic grammar that can and should be augmented by teaching grammar in context, providing consistent feedback on written work, and continually reteaching problem areas.

Final Thoughts

You can't do it alone! Yes, you are a language-arts superstar, but in the end it takes an entire school (and, with luck, an entire family) working in concert over a period of years to develop literate, thoughtful students. As you design your program, an easy first step is introducing a simple set of standards such as the Middle-School Writing Standards that can be found on the CD. After carefully and diplomatically building staff and administrative consensus, share these standards as a voluntary and constructive literacy tool.

Perhaps most important, a teacher who models a playful, open-minded outlook on language can often ignite curiosity or passion about language. As language-arts teachers, our task is to help students begin to see writing conventions as tools, much like a sculptor's chisel or a painter's brush, that give form to beauty and lend clarity to truth. Good luck! ☺

Tips for Success

"A foolish consistency is the hobgoblin of little minds....With consistency a great soul has simply nothing to do. He may as well concern himself with his shadow on the wall."
—Emerson, *Self-Reliance*

Anyone who's taught at a rowdy public school can attest to the value of a steady routine. Daily starters—short lessons used during those often hectic first moments of class—really do help students settle, organize, and engage. Certainly, it's true that students thrive on regularity, yet *Grammar Rulz* aims to steer clear of any "foolish consistency" or "drill and kill" exercises. After all, we aren't trying to awaken the Cyclops of rote memory; to the contrary, we're aiming to quicken curiosity, enliven a willingness to make informed choices, and kindle a lusty enthusiasm for language.

How can I get the most from *Grammar Rulz*?

Grammar Rulz is a daily language program that was designed for use during those potentially chaotic first minutes of class. In addition, the program can be used more intensively by teaching its mini-lessons in clusters rather than single daily exercises. This concentrated method can be particularly effective in classes with multimedia computer projectors or interactive whiteboards. Many teachers align *Grammar Rulz* chapters with social studies units ("Trouble at Vesuvius" with a Roman history unit, for example) throughout the year, but alignment isn't obligatory. Teaching "Anne and the Vikings" *before* a Middle Ages unit provides a great anticipatory set, prior knowledge, and an affective connection; equally, teaching it *after* a Middle Ages unit helps reinforce key concepts and ideas. No matter how you spiral or align the program,

the key principles and practices considered below will help every student achieve success with *Grammar Rulz*.

Never alone! Call students to the board in carefully chosen pairs to make certain that low-skilled or reluctant students have the cover they sometimes need when working in front of the class.

Don't let 'em fail! Keep a running roster to preselect the student pair that will be making corrections in front of the class that day. Provide this pair with focused assistance that will ensure their success at the board.

Character 'TOONs can spark interest in the personalities and storylines that make *Grammar Rulz* fun! Have students read the descriptions aloud and color in the characters during class or for homework. Students are likely to ask many questions; use them as a springboard to generate predictions, create connections, and activate prior knowledge. This short, relaxing activity is an effective pre-reading technique that helps students "get" the story so they can focus on conventions.

Hook 'em! Any material you can use to set the scene—maps, videos, animations, etc.—can serve to activate interest and boost reading comprehension. Use an animation of the Pompeii eruption to hook kids on the "Trouble at Vesuvius" chapter; show a Viking video clip; or prepare a slide show on King Tut's tomb—the possibilities are endless!

Model like a mad dog! Every *Grammar Rulz* chapter is preceded by a sample exercise. Walk students through the steps in the example. Take the time to let them do a high-quality illustration for the vocabulary word. A beautiful model will pay dividends throughout the unit.

It's an art thing! Treat notebook entries and *Grammar Rulz* Express packets as works of art! Banish dull pencils and boring ink. Encourage gel pens and glitter ink—anything that will help students make an affective connection with the work! There's a built-in art extension for each vocabulary word—encourage quality illustrations of a symbolic nature. Require a color illustration as part of the completion grade you give for each packet at the end of a unit. When apt students finish quickly, turn them loose coloring or sketching.

Packet-schmacket! Let students know that the quality and completeness of their notebook or *Grammar Rulz* Express packet is important. Collect it at the end of the unit for completion and effort grades. Save examples to inspire students during upcoming chapters and in years to come!

Set 'em up for success! After students settle in and begin working, read the day's exercise aloud. Use a marker or stylus to circle any areas (comma splices, patterned spelling mistakes, dialogue formatting) that might prove difficult. When working with a PDF, you may choose to identify problem areas directly on the PDF: use the TOOLS > COMMENT & MARKUP > TEXT HIGHLIGHT TOOL or PENCIL TOOL in order to stress areas for student focus. This can be done ahead of time and then undone before students make corrections. On a similar note, Mimio interactive and SMART Board systems both offer a variety of tools with which to emphasize key points.

Lighten up! Your students are already there! Celebrate how much they already know about writing conventions while you work together to sharpen their already impressive skills. Encourage students not to become obsessive about grammar; instead, constantly

remind them that they are studying the language arts, not the language sciences. It's just a little grammar—no big deal.

Don't count beans! Tell students there are *about* twelve corrections in each daily exercise. A flexible number leaves wiggle room for disagreement on disputed points such as the final comma in a list of items. Constantly remind students that writing is an art that involves a series of informed choices rather than any "right" or "wrong" way to express their ideas. It isn't about counting beans; it's about finding opportunities to engage your students in a discussion about language.

Mix and mingle! As students work on the exercise, walk about the classroom offering praise, encouragement, and occasional advice. Circle or highlight areas of focus rather than directly making corrections on student notebooks or packets. Use the word "consider" as you offer clues and hints. Throughout, keep your focus on the pair that will soon come to the board.

Take a swipe! Students sometimes err while making corrections at the board, but now and again you can save the day as they return to their seats. Step close to the board and take a subtle eraser swipe or two before you begin your review! If you do choose to let the mistake stand, ensure you compliment the student's attempt; after all, there's usually a logical reason why they did what they did. Explore and praise their intent before correcting the mistake.

Motivate students with a groovy theme song that plays while they make corrections at the board. If the music's right, the kids will love it! There are even a few catchy songs out there that have to do with the alphabet or vowels.

Schedule review periods periodically (fifteen minutes or so) during which students can clarify troublesome points. One effective method is asking students to highlight each mistake they've corrected in the unit. This can also be a great time to correct missed exercises, finish extension activities, or complete daily vocabulary. Schedule a first review period when you're ten days into a chapter; schedule a second the day before a *Grammar Rulz* Challenge.

Focus on spelling with the My Spelling Gremlins method found on page 89, at the back of *Grammar Rulz* Express packets, or in the Bonus Materials folder on the CD. While using *Grammar Rulz*, encourage students to analyze their spelling mistakes on the My Spelling Gremlins sheet; furthermore, require students to do the same for misspellings made throughout the school day. Guarantee this by making a completed My Spelling Gremlins sheet a part of the final grade given for each chapter.

What is beauty? Though it's difficult to prove empirically, there is a strong connection between the appearance of student work and its underlying quality. When possible, encourage students to drop dull, chewed-up pencil stubs in favor of glorious gel pens. When students begin to like the way their work looks (and remember, this is that rarest moment for many middle-school boys), they naturally tend to have a better affective connection with the project. It's a small matter that can have lasting resonance.

Stand aside! Students tend to stand directly in front of the screen or board while making corrections. Teach them to stand to one side as they correct. At the start of a unit, it's helpful to put on a "good editing" and "bad editing" skit to give students a model.

Leave the notes behind! Reliance on notes slows the correction phase enormously. Ask students to trust themselves and leave their notes behind when they correct at the board.

Put a dictionary atop every student's desk, or, if resources are available, consider desktop electronic versions that create a welcome spike in dictionary use.

Bold, brilliant color makes all the difference when students are correcting at the board or overhead. Buy a bunch of new markers before you start a chapter!

It's like a puzzle—and kids adore puzzles. Present each *Grammar Rulz* exercise as a pleasant game of grammatical hide and seek. Twelve errors are hidden in the woodwork—seek them out!

Save time on Brain Blaster extensions by having a pair of students work at the board while others work at their seats.

Hang posters! SUPER PROOFER proofreading symbols can be found on the CD and page xx. If you want to enlarge the SUPER PROOFER poster past the 11 x 17-inch size your copy center can offer, consider seeing your tech specialist for instructions on how to print posters on multiple sheets of paper that students can cut and tape together to form a mega-poster.

Allow for differences! Dialect, vernacular, idiom, local usage, and regional accents act to enrich to our language—and what a loss it is when we attempt to smother everything non-standard. Teachers should always seek to broaden rather than homogenize language, so it may be better to respect the sometimes rough-cut language of our students while always searching for ways to help them develop a more standard English they can call upon when the situation requires.

Frequent Comments/Questions

Their Question: "I rewrote the sentence this way. Is that okay?"

Your Answer: "There are many wonderful ways to rewrite this sentence, and you've done a first-rate job. However, for these exercises, just try to fix what's wrong with small changes in spelling, capitalization, punctuation, grammar, and usage. Resist the temptation to rewrite whole sentences—just fix what's broken!"

Their Question: "Is that an extra space between the 'j' and the 'a' over there? You know, where it says a jar?"
Your Answer: "No, the font's just crazy like that. It's just a goofy little quirk. Don't worry about it!"

Their Question: "Why do I have to use color?"
Your Answer: "Why did they (mainly) stop making black and white movies? Why does your computer screen display bazillions of colors? Why isn't every building on the street painted gray?"

Their Question: "Why do I have to fix sentences that are poorly written?"
Your Answer: "Editing is part of the writing process. It's what we do to our own writing, and it's what we do as we help peers to improve their work. Heck, you can even get a job as an editor at a newspaper, website, or magazine."

Their Question: "Why do I have to draw a picture of the word in this stupid picture frame thing? I suck at drawing."
Your Answer: "Hey, I know what you mean, but, believe it or not, we're not after the illustration—we're trying to get you to think about the meaning of the word. When we create an original illustration of an idea, our minds make bazillions of connections with the word's meaning. We're trying to get you to think by drawing. Try to be symbolic rather than representative. If the word of the day is *duel*, you might draw crossed swords instead of a whole scene. That'll help you remember the meaning."

Assessment

Each *Grammar Rulz* chapter provides a variety of opportunities to assess your students. Two *Grammar Rulz* Challenges—short, easy-to-grade quizzes—are embedded within each chapter. In addition, *Grammar Rulz* Express packets or notebooks can be carefully assessed to provide another view of student learning.

***Grammar Rulz* Challenges** each contain ten mistakes. The required corrections are based on the material students have just covered. Challenge #1 covers the first half of the chapter. Challenge #2 is based on the second half of the chapter. You can, however, fairly ask students to review the entire chapter before Challenge #2 because a few errors will have been addressed in both halves of the chapter. *Grammar Rulz* Express packets have markers placed midway through each chapter to remind students and teachers of an impending assessment.

Preparing for a *Grammar Rulz* Challenge is easy. Schedule the first review session about ten days into the chapter. Schedule a second the day before the test date. Ask students to review notebook entries or *Grammar Rulz* Express packets by carefully highlighting each mistake they've corrected since the beginning of the chapter or, in the case of Challenge #2, their last challenge. This is also a great time for students to catch up on missing work, fill in missing Grammar Boy rules, complete Brain Blaster exercises, illustrate/define vocabulary words, add words to the My Spelling Gremlins list, and, importantly, to ask clarifying questions. Students can take home their notebooks or packets to study. You may also consider giving review work in troublesome areas that will appear on an upcoming challenge.

Two versions of each *Grammar Rulz* Challenge let you provide varying levels of support for your students. Challenges #1A and #2A are modified with red boxes that highlight ten areas students should consider when making corrections. These modified challenges offer sometimes-needed extra support. In addition, it may be helpful to briefly display Challenge #1A or #2A as students correct the unmodified version.

Review challenges as you would any daily exercise, but ask each student to make just a single correction. It's helpful to call less apt students to the board first to give them a higher chance at success. You can even stack the cards in their favor by subtly pointing out a correction you'd like them to make before they head to the board. Self-grading offers many advantages. Require students to put aside the pen with which they corrected the test in favor of a highlighter for self-correcting. Once the grading is done, individualizing your instruction becomes critical. Consider reteaching in areas of weakness like setting off names in direct address, capitalizing proper adjectives, etc. Stay positive by letting students know that mastering writing conventions is a process that takes years, not weeks.

Notebooks or *Grammar Rulz* Express packets can be easily graded by creating a simple completion rubric that matches the elements you've been stressing throughout the chapter. Consider requiring completion of two My Spelling Gremlins sheets for each unit.

Throw 'em a curve! Mastering conventions is a process, so it may be wise to deduct five points (rather than ten) for each error on a challenge, at least during the early innings. ☺

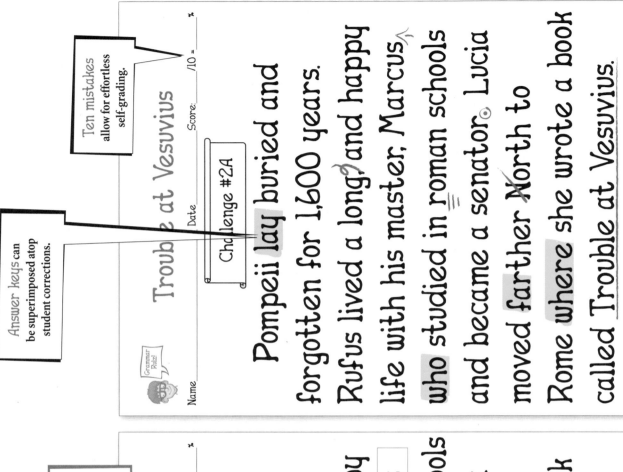

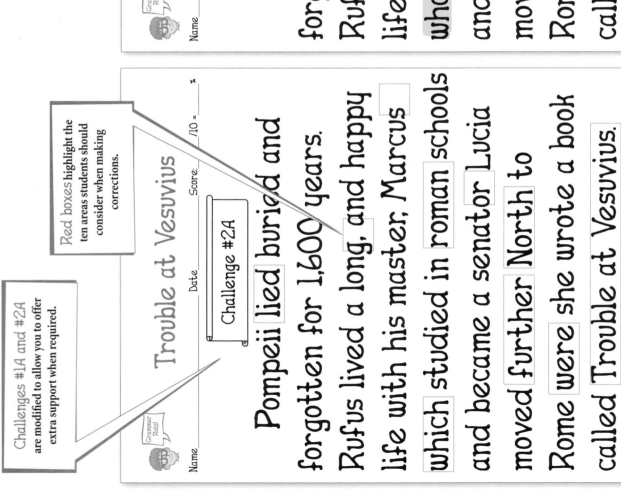

Challenges #1B and #2B are unmodified, allowing for more rigorous testing.

Errors are based on the material covered in the preceding half of the chapter

Name _____ Date _____ Score: _____ /10 = _____ %

Trouble at Vesuvius

Challenge #2B

Pompeii lied buried and forgotten for 1,600 years. Rufus lived a long, and happy life with his master, Marcus which studied in roman schools and became a senator Lucia moved further North to Rome were she wrote a book called Trouble at Vesuvius.

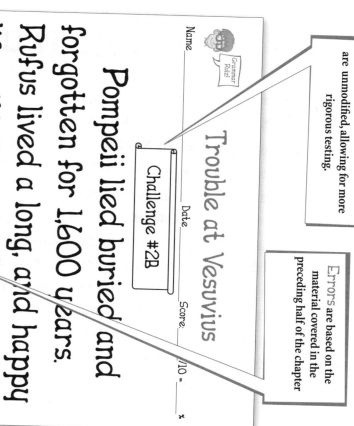

Answer keys can be superimposed atop student corrections.

Ten mistakes allow for effortless self-grading.

Name _____ Date _____ Score: _____ /10 = _____ %

Trouble at Vesuvius

Challenge #2B

Pompeii lay buried and forgotten for 1,600 years. Rufus lived a long and happy life with his master, Marcus, who studied in roman schools and became a senator. Lucia moved farther North to Rome where she wrote a book called Trouble at Vesuvius.

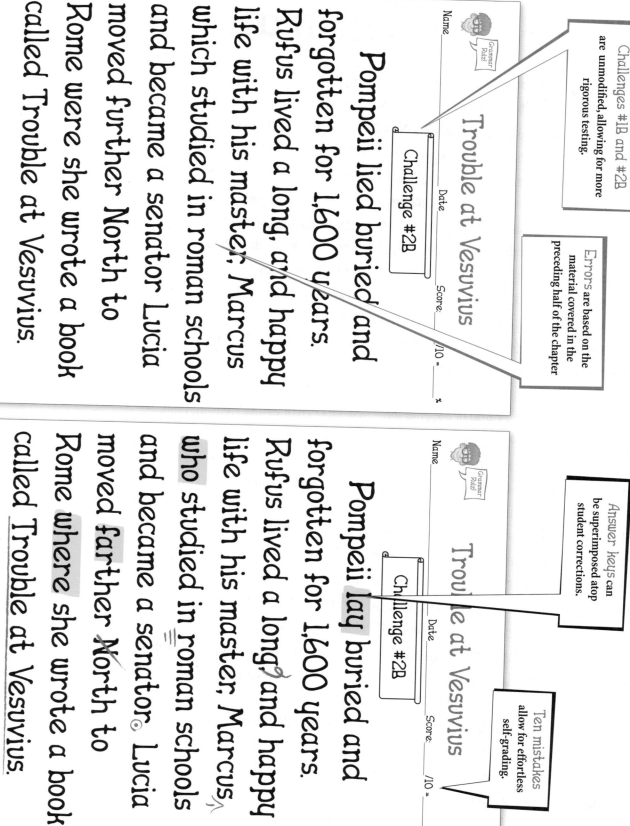

Bibliography

Baines, John, and Jaromir Malek. <u>Atlas of Ancient Egypt</u>. New York: Facts on File, 1989.

Bisel, Sara C. <u>The Secrets of Vesuvius</u>. New York: Scholastic, 1990.

Clayton, Peter. <u>Chronicle of the Pharaohs</u>. New York: Thames and Hudson, 1994.

Connolly, Peter. <u>Pompeii</u>. Oxford: Oxford University Press, 1990.

Crystal, David. <u>The Cambridge Biographical Encyclopedia</u>. Cambridge: Cambridge UP, 1994.

Crystal, David. <u>The Cambridge Encyclopedia</u>. 3rd ed. Cambridge: Cambridge UP, 1997.

Crystal, David. <u>The Cambridge Encyclopedia of the English Language</u>. Cambridge: Cambridge UP, 1996.

D'Aulaire, Ingri and Edgar. <u>Book of Greek Myths</u>. New York: Doubleday, 1962.

Ellsworth, Blanche. <u>English Simplified.</u> Thomas E. Crowell Company, Inc. 1977.

<u>Emerson's Prose and Poetry</u>. New York: W.W. Norton and Company, 2001.

Goor, Ron and Nancy. <u>Pompeii</u>. New York: Thomas Crowell, 1986.

<u>Grammar and Composition</u>. 3rd ed. Englewood Cliffs, NJ: Prentice-Hall, 1987.

<u>Grammar and Composition Handbook</u>. New York: Glencoe, 2000.

<u>Harbrace College Handbook</u>. 11th ed.. San Diego: Harcourt Brace, 1990.

Hobson, Christine. <u>The World of the Pharaohs</u>. New York: Thames and Hudson, 1990.

Johnson, Paul. <u>The Civilization of Ancient Egypt</u>. New York: Harper Collins, 1999.

Kamm, Anthony. <u>The Romans</u>. London: Routledge, 1997.

Mellor, Ronald , and Marni McGee. <u>The Ancient Roman World</u>. Oxford: Oxford University Press, 2004.

<u>Merriam-Webster's Collegiate Dictionary</u>. 11th ed.. Springfield, Mass.: Merriam-Webster Inc., 2003.

Murdoch, David. <u>Tutankhamun</u>. New York: DK Publishing, 1998.

Nardo, Don. <u>Life in Ancient Rome</u>. San Diego: Lucent Books, 1997.

<u>New Merriam-Webster Dictionary</u>. Springfield, Mass.: Merriam-Webster Inc., 1989.

Patent, Dorothy Hinshaw. <u>Lost City of Pompeii</u>. Tarrytown, NY: Benchmark Books, 2000.

Pearson, Anne. <u>Ancient Greece</u>. New York: DK Publishing, 2004.

Reeves, Nicholas. <u>The Complete Tutankhamun</u>. New York: Thames and Hudson, 1990.

Roehrig, Catherine. <u>Fun with Hieroglyphics</u>. New York: Metropolitan Museum of Art, 1990.

Simons, Gerald. <u>Barbarian Europe</u>. New York: Time-Life, 1968.

Shertzer, Margaret. <u>The Elements of Grammar</u>. New York: Collier Books, 1986.

<u>Student Atlas of the World</u>. Washington, DC: National Geographic Society.

Truss, Lynne. <u>Eats, Shoots & Leaves</u>. New York: Gotham Books, 2003.

<u>Webster's New World Dictionary</u>. New York: Warner Books, 1990.

Wernick, Robert. <u>The Vikings</u>. Alexandria, VA: Time-Life, 1979.

Wood, Michael. <u>The Dark Ages</u>. New York: Facts on File, 1987.

<u>Write Source 2000</u>. Boston: Write Source, 1995.

My Spelling Gremlins

Gremlin ?	Bust it up!	Break it down!	Say it!	Jot it x 2!	Mnemonic
Dispossessed	Dis pos sessed	Base-possess Prefix-dis Suffix-ed	X	• dispossessed • dispossessed	Possess possesses four S's!
		Base- Prefix- Suffix-		..	
		Base- Prefix- Suffix-		..	
		Base- Prefix- Suffix-		..	
		Base- Prefix- Suffix-		..	
		Base- Prefix- Suffix-		..	
		Base- Prefix- Suffix-		..	
		Base- Prefix- Suffix-		..	
		Base- Prefix- Suffix-		..	